A Beginner's Guide to
House Plants

Ryusuke Sakaino

TUTTLE Publishing

Tokyo | Rutland, Vermont | Singapore

CONTENTS

OUTDOORS

FULL SUN

PARTIAL SHADE

Why I Wrote This Book

All kinds of things and circumstances shape our lives. Those that we select ourselves enrich our day to day living. This book is aimed at people who want to incorporate really good things that help them live life in their own unique way. We've summarized the basic knowledge in graphical form that makes it fun to choose plants, containers and tools, and work with the ideas for how to use them. This book is filled with hints on how to find plants and settings for them that are really "you," and not just plants and pots you've happened to acquire.

The presence of houseplants enriches our lives. In this book, with the help of many Japanese growers and shop owners, we cover not only recommended houseplants, but ideas for stylishly incorporating them into interiors, the basics of their cultivation for people who always end up killing plants, and so on. We hope it will help you to live a green life that is uniquely your own.

—Ryusuke Sakaino

Creating a Life with More Greenery

So you want to bring more plants into your life and
have bought some, but they just don't look right…
Starting with Ryusuke Sakaino, from the plant shop AYANAS, we've
asked various shop owners, makers and artists for tips and ideas that
can help you create a beautiful and stylish environment.

Selecting Your Plants

A house where plants grow cultivates people, too!

Plants bring color to interior spaces. Do them the favor of not forgetting that they are living things as well as decorations for a room. Consider carefully where they are placed. When I choose a room for a plant, my must-have condition is that the room gets good sunlight and ventilation. These are prerequisites for growing healthy plants. A sunny spot is a matter of course, but even more important is ventilation. A room where fresh air can circulate is good for people, and it's also good for plants. It is, of course, not possible to move house for the sake of plants, but keep in mind that sunlight and ventilation are important for both people and plants.

Decide where it will be placed, then choose the plant!

Take a good look at your space. While there may be windows where sunlight streams in, there are probably also places that don't get much natural light. The temperature, level of humidity and sunlight that a plant prefers depend on its natural habitat. Some like strong light, while others prefer very humid, dark environments. Try to place the plant somewhere that is as close to its natural habitat as possible.

In the plant catalog in this book, we have listed as a guide the three types of places that suit various plants (see page 108), with 1) being an outdoor environment or balcony that receives direct sunlight, 2) a bright indoor environment that receives plenty of sunlight, such as near a window and 3) a semi-lit indoor environment, such as somewhere that may be in shade but receives enough light by which to read a newspaper. Please refer to this when choosing plants and where to place them.

For Your First Plant, Choose Something Easy

Sansevieria come from dry, arid regions. Their entire body stores water, so it's fine not to water them very often. The varieties in the photo are Sansevieria banana and Sansevieria cylindrica. They store water in their thick leaves.

Varieties that require infrequent watering

If you're wanting to welcome some new plants after moving house or to make a start at living with greenery, you might be wondering what to look for. If you really don't want to make mistakes, why not start with plants that are suitable for beginners? It's difficult to say what makes a plant easy to grow, but from the point of view that they don't need much looking after, plants that require watering only infrequently are easy to cultivate. In this regard, I recommend Sansevieria. Plants with thick leaves are particularly good at storing water, so it's fine not to water them too often, meaning that even people who are busy and are not confident they will be able to care for them properly can grow them with ease.

Plants in the family Araceae are classic houseplants. Many varieties in this family are highly shade tolerant (meaning they can withstand a lack of sunlight), with the pothos being the classic example. They're often seen in shops or offices where natural light is hard to come by. The photos below show two varieties of Philodendron oxycardium, which have adorable heart shaped leaves. They grow well in semi-shade.

Schefflera are robust plants that cope well with a lack of sunlight and don't readily pose problems. For these reasons, you'll often see them at public facilities and offices. This one has been trained into a slightly unusual shape.

Shade tolerant, sturdy plants

If you think "ease of cultivation" is the same thing as "resistance to dying," the classic pothos and other plants in the Araceae family are good options. They do like sunny spots, but are highly tolerant of shade (they have the ability to withstand a lack of sunlight) so can be grown in living environments, offices, shops and so on that don't get much sun. Schefflera (page 133) are also highly shade tolerant. They are a standard houseplant, so many people will be familiar with them. There are many species of Schefflera with interesting trunk formations or that can be trained in interesting ways, so look for one that you like.

Choosing a Plant for Your Tabletop

Readily available plants for tabletops

Small potted plants are readily available and make easy interior accents. Placing several of them together on a table, kitchen counter, the side of a desk and so on instantly creates a lively atmosphere in a dull room. Recently, they have become available at discount department stores as well as home improvement stores. Pachira, Ficus macrocarpa, Chamaedorea elegans, Fraxinus japonica and so on are often sold as small plants. They are all easy to grow varieties that can be welcomed into a room with no hesitation. In my shop, the classic mini plant is the Dischidia (see page 139). The table-top sized version is popular as it is so easy to care for. It also works well as a small gift.

Living with small plants for longer periods

Small pot plants don't take up much room and are easy to group together. However, there are a few things to keep in mind. Firstly, as the pots they are planted in are small, so is the amount of soil in the pots, which means the soil tends to dry out. Don't forget to check the condition of the soil and water them! Furthermore, although the plants are in small pots, they are not all small plant varieties. For example, in its natural environment, Ficus macrocarpa grows to tens of feet/meters in height. Remember that the plant is a living thing, so although it is small when you buy it, it will grow bigger over time. On the other hand, one of the enjoyable things about plants is observing their growth when you live with them for a long period.

Looking for a "Symbol Tree"*

Big and tall: a tree with presence

A "symbol tree" originally called to mind a large tree in the garden of a house, but it could also be a "symbol tree in a living room." In addition to large potted plants, try hanging a large Platycerium bifurcatum (elkhorn fern) or other plants with a strong presence to make them play a leading role in a room. Some people may think that as they end up killing even small plants, they won't have any luck with large ones, but in many cases it is the large plants that are strong and robust. You could even start with large potted plants. The longer they live with you, the more they will become part of your life and the more attached to them you will become. They will become a symbol of your house in the real sense of the word.

* In Japan, this is a tree that's symbolic of a house, a public building such as a railway station, a city or neighborhood, etc. It's a real pleasure to choose a plant that particularly reflects you and your home.

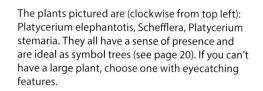

The plants pictured are (clockwise from top left): Platycerium elephantotis, Schefflera, Platycerium stemaria. They all have a sense of presence and are ideal as symbol trees (see page 20). If you can't have a large plant, choose one with eyecatching features.

Keep the Shape of the Plant in Mind

No two plants are shaped exactly alike

Purchasing plants over the internet has become common. The question is whether you'll receive the item you saw in the photo online. Take as an example the various Ficus benghalensis on the opposite page. Although they are the same plant, they each have individual differences in terms of their branches, leaves and overall balance. If you're going to the effort of welcoming a plant into your home, you want to choose one with a shape that works for you. Many online stores sell the actual items depicted in their photos, making it possible to choose the plant shape that you like. However there are many appealing aspects and discoveries that don't come across in photos and can only be realized by actually handling the plant, so find some stores you like and pay them a visit.

One plant, six shapes—bear in mind that when buying online, the plant you receive may not exactly match the one you saw on screen. If shape or orientation is a concern, it's best to visit a nursery, where what you see is what you get.

Pay Attention to Leaf Shape and Color

Ornamental plants are all about the leaves

Houseplants are also called ornamental plants, and each is ornamental in its own way. Let's take a look at the characteristics of the leaves, such as their shapes, colors, patterns and textures. The leaf shape is a major element when choosing plants, whether it is cute and round or pointy and stylish. There are big leaves, small leaves, long and narrow leaves and leaves shaped like hearts. Start with the leaves to find a plant that you like. The impression they make is a factor that can't be ignored when considering their compatibility with your décor. The characteristically shaped leaves of plants such as monstera can also be enjoyed for the shadows they cast on the floor. Try incorporating attractive dappled light into your interior design.

The relationship between leaves and room size

Plants with big leaves such as monstera, pachira and Ficus umbellata take up a large amount of space, so it's possible to create a sense of presence with just one plant. On the other hand, plants with loosely spaced, delicate leaves can be placed in confined spaces and small studio-type dwellings without overwhelming them. When placing several small potted plants together, pay attention to the shape of the leaves. For example, putting plants together that have differently shaped leaves highlights the characteristics of each plant. If they appear disjointed, create a cohesive look by using pots of the same hue, shape or material.

What are Unusual "Exotic Plants"?

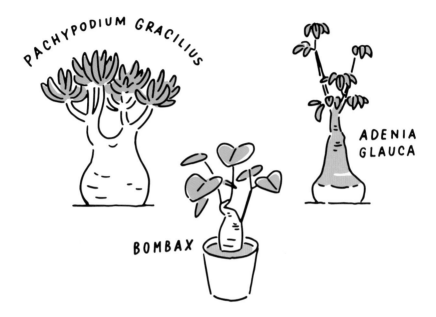

PACHYPODIUM GRACILIUS

ADENIA GLAUCA

BOMBAX

The world of highly collectible tuberous plants

For those wanting something unconventional and individualistic, try a caudex plant. These are tuberous plants with uniquely shaped bases. Caudex lovers form a microcosm. It's a world where many people have large collections, as collecting rare items stimulates the appetite for more. In this book, we cover plants representative of caudex types, including Pachypodium gracilis (see page 148) and Bombax ellipticum (page 168).

Look for unusual form in a readily available variety

Even among the popular varieties that are distributed in large volumes, it's possible to find individual examples of plants trained into interesting shapes. Types that extend their branches upward can be tied with cord so that the branches stretch out horizontally; bases and roots can be intentionally raised above the ground (see page 28). Various techniques can give even common, familiar plants a fresh, novel appearance, such as growing a tree over several years in a pot tilted on an angle to disorient it in terms of up and down, thereby disrupting its shape. Unusual plants are the result of chance meetings and fate. Make frequent visits to stores and check online shops regularly. As plants develop even after purchase, there is also the joy of shaping them yourself, as you would a bonsai.

Enjoying Aerial Roots and Fasciations

The pleasure of admiring roots

Have you ever seen the huge Ficus macrocarpa trees also known as "Indian Laurel" and "Curtain Fig?" I'm sure some of you will be familiar with the roots that flow down like a beard from a large, round trunk. Those roots are called aerial roots. They extend down as the tree grows, aiming for the ground. Many people appreciate these trees for their mysterious, unique form. The Philodendron kookaburra and other varieties of philodendron are representative of varieties that can be appreciated for their aerial roots, but there are also some types in circulation which don't grow aerial roots but can be trained so that their roots are visible. This type of shaping is called *ne-agari* (exposed root) and is considered to be one of the ways to enjoy bonsai and other ornamental plants.

The exposed root balances the lush, broad foliage and long slender trunk.

Fasciation can be caused by a number of factors—temperature, insects and crowding are some natural causes, but applied factors such as light and nutrition control, wounding at the growing point and other actions can create this phenomenon. The waving and cresting (cristation) you see here happens when the plant veers off from its vertical pattern and becomes more horizontal.

FORMA CRISTATA

Enjoying the unique appearance created by fasciation

Have you ever seen strawberries or vegetables with distorted shapes? This phenomenon is called fasciation and it occurs when there are mutations in the growing tips. It can occur in some varieties of houseplants, and is particularly common in succulents and cacti, which have long been known for their individuality. If you buy a regular tree, even if you choose one shaped to your liking, in five to ten years its shape will resemble others. But in the case of fasciation, even cacti of the same variety will completely alter in appearance over time and their overall balance will be completely different. I believe that the appeal of fasciation lies in not knowing how the plant will turn out.

When choosing a plant, consider the space you are trying to fill, the available light in the space, and what you hope the plant will contribute—bright color? Interesting shape and form? A sense of harmony and continuity?

Living With Succulents and Cacti

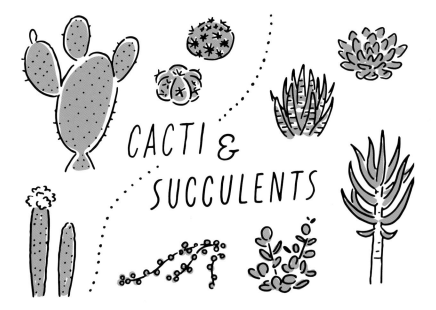

Unique forms that have evolved to suit their environments

Many people are attracted by the adorable appearance of succulents and have one or two in their homes. We asked TOKIIRO, a designer of succulent arrangements, about the appeal of succulents, which we don't know much about despite their seeming so familiar.

"There are thousands of varieties of succulents. Common to all of them is that they store water in their leaves, stems and inside their roots. They mainly originate from arid regions in Latin America and southern Africa. Their appearance, which has evolved in response to their harsh environment, contributes significantly to their appeal. There are some plants you wish you could ask 'why did you become that color or shape?'. In Japan, they've been popular for horticultural use since the Edo period. Part of their charm lies in their leaves changing color in line with Japan's four seasons."

Succulents love the sun. Actually, many varieties are not suited to being indoor plants. Place them outside, such as on the balcony or in the garden, or if keeping them indoors, make sure they are somewhere that gets direct sunlight. If they don't get sufficient light, they will become spindly, meaning they will grow long and gangly. If this happens, move them somewhere else. It's also important that—just as for other plants—they are placed somewhere with good ventilation. In terms of watering, it depends on the type and the environment in which they are situated, but as a guide, water them every two weeks when the soil has dried out, giving them enough water so that it runs out from the hole in the pot base. People tend to think that succulents don't need watering, but they love water. They can store water in their leaves, and giving them too much causes water overload, so give them less than other plants.

Arranging Succulents

A little universe of succulents in a container

"At TOKIIRO we create various arrangements using succulents. We plant them like bouquets in little containers or place many varieties together to create a forest in an artisan-made ceramic container with undulations. A deep, rich world is born in a small vessel.

Succulents can also be used to make wreaths. TOKIIRO got its start with these wreaths. They are made up of living succulents to decorate walls. Extrapolating from the wreaths, we make tableaux from sphagnum moss and boards. People enjoy the changes in these three-dimensional pictures that grow over time. Apart from this, if they are planted in a hanging container, succulents can also be hung up for display. One of the major attractions of succulents is that they can be arranged freely like this."

A tall mug can house a low-growing arrangement, but can also handle inclusion of a taller plant, striking a nice balance.

Small group plantings like these are perfect for small spaces.

Little forest-like universes grow in small containers in these arrangements by TOKIIRO. Try making a base hole in your favorite small vessel and create group plantings. Detailed steps are on page 76.

Displaying Your Plants

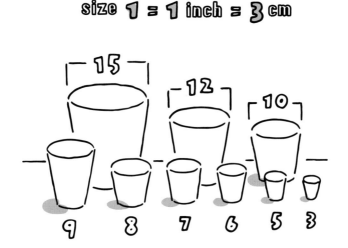

size 1 = 1 inch = 3 cm

15

12

10

9   8   7   6   5   3

Choosing plant pots and the size of outer containers

Plant pot sizes are represented by numbers. Size 1 is about 1¼" (3 cm) in diameter and height. The number is determined by the diameter at the pot's widest section, with a pot with diameter of 9½" (24 cm) being a size 8. While they may have the same number, pots can be different heights, with short ones known as shallow pots and tall ones known as deep pots. If you are putting a plant pot so that it fits snugly inside an outer pot, take care with the size. If the outer pot is too large or deep, the soil in the plant pot inside it will not get any light and as air can't get in, it will cause the soil to grow moldy. For large, heavy potted plants, we recommend outer pots with casters. This is helpful in situations where the pot needs to be moved often due to cleaning, a shop layout and so on.

Basket

Pot Cover

Pot

Appearance? Function? Choosing plant pots and materials

Plant pots are an important part of interior design. Plants need to be comfortable in them and they also need to look good. At the time of purchase, most plants are in plastic pots or black plastic containers. They can't be said to be stylish, but in terms of plant growth, plastic is not a bad material, so there's no real need for repotting after purchase. From a design perspective, it's possible to conceal them with an outer pot, which may be something like a woven basket or ceramic vessel with no hole in the base. Plant pots come in various materials such as ceramics, concrete, metal and wood. Purely in terms of the plant, unglazed terracotta is the best material. It has the advantage of allowing air to circulate and not allowing roots to get too cold even during winter watering.

Have Fun Looking for Pots and Containers

Shapes, materials, colors, sizes, pairings with plants: The possibilities are endless!

Try to find the perfect pot and outer pot to suit your interior décor. Enjoy the balance between the plant and the pot as you would when looking for crockery or a vessel for your favorite dish. Recently, there are a lot of free-form options, so there is no end of possibilities in terms of matching the shape of plants with pots. If you feel it will be too difficult to repot the plant yourself, look for a shop that sells plants that are already in pots that you like. Here, we list examples of various plant pots and outer pots. Please use them as a reference when putting together your interior design. Please note that stock levels in any given store will vary from time to time, so visit stores' websites, if applicable, to confirm what is available.

Here we offer examples from Japanese stores that have contributed to this book. Each shows interesting and creative ways to give your plant a healthy home and make the most of its beauty. If you wish to visit them or check out their websites, you'll find their information starting on page 189.

AYANAS

AYANAS favors pots that are designed to blend in with interior decor and are easy to use from a horticultural point of view. The elusive simplicity and ease of use of these items explain their appeal.

SNARK

Architectural firm SNARK favors steel for both outer containers and direct planting. Well- designed, interestingly colored steel containers work well with industrial decor.

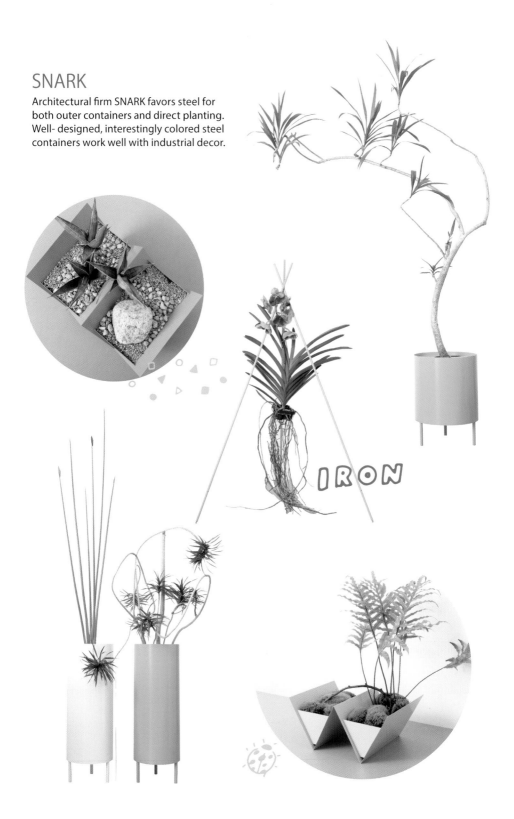

IRON

HACHILABO

When choosing a pot, you have to consider the plant's personality as well as its needs. Simple pots can be too bland, but overly elaborate ones are difficult to match with plants. These pots from HACHILABO are designed to strike the right balance with pots that are richly nuanced in color and texture.

aarde

These examples from aarde, an online store set up by long-established plant pot wholesaler Oumi Touki, show a bit of the variety a specialty story can offer. By checking out these places, either in your area or on the internet, you'll discover many options you didn't know existed. You and your plant will be living with the container for a long time, so don't settle for anything that doesn't really make you happy. Take your time to explore the infinite variety that's out there.

ROUSSEAU

These terrariums by ROUSSEAU show you how unique these plant habitats can be. There is a poetic quality to these glass polyhedrons, which appear to be made from mineral crystals. A purpose-made terrarium doesn't have to be confined to plantings. Try using one as a vase for flowers.

Flying

The number of things that can serve as stylish and healthy homes for plants might surprise you. Here Flying shows you how epiphyte boards can be shaped to display Platycerium bifurcatum (elkhorn ferns), and very unlikely-looking structures can house kokedama. Resources for creative display are everywhere.

menui

The woven basketry suits a wide range of interior looks, such as natural, Asian, shabby chic, Scandinavian and country-style, so definitely give them a go as outer pots. Here, menui shows examples of baskets from different parts of the world. And, again, we see how metal can complement plants beautifully, as in the case of this hanging metal basket and watering can.

ideot

Encasing a pot in rich fabric is a brilliant idea—a great way to design your own container. These pots from ideot are covered in "old gabbeh," traditional carpets handwoven by Iranian nomadic peoples. Mixing textures and finishes, as you see in the pots far below, is another way to add dimension.

Gather Plants Together in a Sunny Spot

Turn a sunny windowside into a premium spot for plants

Sun and ventilation are important for plants, but that doesn't mean they can only be grown in rooms where the sun is shining on them. Realistically, you have to find the best environment possible for them wherever you are living currently. To do this, we recommend displaying plants grouped together where there is the most sunlight. If they are in pots, they can be placed by a window, or for small plants, make special designated high seats for them by placing a table or stool somewhere sunny. When considering the placement of interior items and furniture, it's best to start out by putting a "special plant table" or shelf by the window that gets the most light. If you want to live with greenery for a long time, think "plants first!"

Create a designated space to gather plants

If your plants are scattered throughout the house, try condensing them in one spot. Doing this means they can all be cared for at once, and as they are easier to see, you are less likely to forget about them. If you have a big window that lets in plenty of light, we recommend placing them together by the window where the sun's rays will reach them. Even if there are only a few plants, making one wall into a plant space will reinforce the impression of your house as a "house with greenery." It's the same as a bouquet making more of an impression than individual flowers. Rearranging the plants with little accessories and objects depending on your mood is fun, too.

Decorative Shelves Can Create a Garden Look

Ladder Shelf

High shelves maximize sunlight

On the previous pages we talked about giving plants premium seats, and one way to make sure the precious sunlight entering the room reaches as many plants as possible is to use high decorative shelving. Gathering the plants on the shelving gives one corner of the room the air of botanical gardens. In the house I lived in previously, I placed high shelving dedicated to plants next to a window. The key point when using high shelves is to incorporate plants with trailing leaves. Adding plants with long, trailing vines such as Dischidia and Rhipsalis creates variation and brings depth to the space. Open shelving, ladders and ladder shelving such as stepladders also make good decorative shelves.

Winding a vine around a post, incorporating plants with trailing leaves, and so on, prevent a display from becoming dull. This display uses Stephanotis floribunda and Dischidia.

Ornamental shelving using a wooden box. Shelving is also useful when you want to create different heights. (box from Midori no Zakkaya)

Keep Height Differences in Mind

Create variations in height through plant size and shelving

One of the tricks to displaying plants is to be conscious of height differences. For example, if you have two or three potted plants on the floor, put one on a stool or mini table. Even when you have many small plants on shelves, make sure that their pots are different heights. Using a pot plant stand is also a good idea, and hanging plants from high up is also effective in creating variation (see page 68). We also recommend creating variation by bringing plants of different sizes together. As in the illustration on the left, place three plants of different sizes in a triangular formation. Simply keeping a triangular shape in mind will create balance.

Place upward-facing plants in a lower position

Have you ever been aware of plants' "faces?" Plants definitely have angles from which they look their best. We call the part of the plant viewed from this angle the "face." For example, Agaves have upturned faces, and look best from directly above, or in a "bird's-eye view composition." Keep the display height low for this type of plant, such as lined up together on top of a cabinet at waist height. In terms of the small items placed among the plants, it's a good idea to choose things that have a pleasing shape when viewed from above. Finding plants that suit your interior in this way is part of the fun.

Creating Your "Dream Green" Interior

Be conscious of differences in look and form when combining items

A house full of plants is something to aspire to, isn't it? Once you're used to selecting and caring for plants, you'll want to fill the house with them to create a green interior all of your own. Asian resort-style, full of tropical varieties. A collection of rare plants for a masculine interior look. Foliage plants with a sense of warmth for a Scandinavian interior. Plants all carry with them the air of their place of origin, so try to incorporate the image that they give off into your interior design. When displaying many plants together, try intentionally grouping many with the same form or combining types with differently oriented leaves for a complex, jungle-like space. Enjoy creating arrangements with a sense of rhythm.

Displaying Plants Like Pictures

Flying Plants

An original epiphyte board designed by product design company Flying.
(Available at Flying/see page 189 for shop details)

Hang plants on a wall as you would display pictures

Try hanging plants on the wall as you would display pictures. For epiphytes such as orchids, ferns, air plants and other plants that attach themselves to trees and rocks, as long as the material to which they are attaching can be permeated by water and air and can retain moisture, just about anything is fine. Tree fern backing boards, driftwood and volcanic rock are all common and have long been customized for use by farmers and horticulturalists. These customized items can be hung from a wall. Recently, items such as highly designed epiphyte boards have given rise to a new sense of value from an interior and product design perspective. We've been seeing them in stores a lot more than previously, so why not give them a try? The instructions for attaching the plant to the board are on page 79.

Balcony Gardening

Choose plants that suit an outdoor environment

If you'd love to create a garden to your own taste but live in an apartment, balcony gardening is an attractive option. With some ingenuity, even a small area can be made into a space full of originality. Although plants love sunlight, you'll need to take care selecting plants that can stand up to intense summer heat and light. Under the scorching rays of the sun and with the high temperatures caused by reflection of light, balconies tend to create harsh environments. Therefore, choose plants that will grow even in these conditions. Succulents such as cacti and aloe tolerate direct sunlight well and are suited to being kept on balconies. Other plants suited to outdoor environments are marked with an "outdoor symbol" in the catalog in this book, for easy reference.

Small Balcony Garden

This is the balcony of RIKA, a balcony garden creator (see page 94).

Measures against winter cold and intense heat

As a balcony is not as readily within eyesight as indoor spaces are, one tends to water and care for plants less. Choose succulents, cacti, aloe and so on that can tolerate a lack of water. That said, direct sunlight tends to dry out soil, so don't let them go too long without water as the soil will dry out completely. In summer, make sure the air conditioner doesn't blow directly on your plants. If the sun is too strong, use netting to create shade. The cold of winter is very stressful for plants from tropical regions. Bring types that are vulnerable to cold indoors over winter. If the floor is concrete, dramatic differences in temperature can be ameliorated by laying down decking made from cork or wood.

Various Ways to Display Air Plants

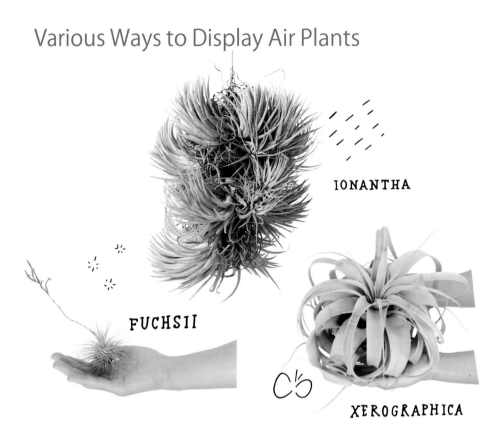

IONANTHA

FUCHSII

XEROGRAPHICA

Super-popular air plants

Tillandsia are epiphytes that don't require soil. Also known as air plants, they are widely popular as they can be placed almost anywhere. In their original habitat, they attach themselves to large trees or rocks and take in moisture through their leaves and entire body structure in order to grow. For this reason, they don't need to take root in soil and can be grown inside containers or in various other places and displayed in the same way as interior objects. With their mysterious appearance unlike that of a potted plant, air plants have a unique, characteristic presence. Indoors, they like well-ventilated places with soft light like that filtered through lace curtains or semi-shade with just enough light to read a newspaper. There are hundreds of varieties, so why not give air plants a try?

They can be displayed in a variety of places

One of the major attractions of air plants is the huge variety of ways they can be displayed. They look great placed in a glass vessel or a basket, or even placed randomly among other items on an ornamental shelf. Large ones can be hung from the ceiling, and they can even be hung from a wall like dried flowers. As they are light, they can be suspended from the branches of large potted plants or from curtain rails—basically, they can be displayed anywhere. Furthermore, as they are hygienic in the sense that they don't require soil, they are perfect for places that you don't want made dirty, such as the dining table or around the kitchen. They are chosen for shop displays and office plantings for this reason. Wherever you display them, though, don't forget to make sure that air can circulate.

Tillandsia

Glass containers work well with air plants. Place them inside a little glass dome as a terrarium or display them inside a hanging container. Just make sure not to seal the container and check that air is circulating around them.

Air plants are light, so can be hung anywhere. Hang them from the branch of a large plant for a unique look.

Air Plants

Covering the surface of potted plants' soil with ornamental stones or woodchips is called mulching. Apart from the horticultural advantage of preventing soil from drying out and keeping pests away, it has the effect of enhancing the interior design of a room. Using air plants as mulching makes for an attractive accent. The plant is covered with trichomes (the fine hair-like structures on the leaf surface) which shine brightly in the sunlight.

Creating a Moss Terrarium

GREEN LIFE

A little forest in glass that is soothing to look at

Terrariums using moss are popular at the moment as this greenery requires little effort. We spoke to moss terrarium artist and workshop facilitator Mr. Kawamoto from Feel The Garden about them. "People want houseplants but don't have room, or don't have good sunlight. Or they have small children or pets, so are worried about having soil in the house. They may be busy and not have time to water. For people with these constraints, I suggest terrariums using moss. In an airtight glass jar, moss, sand, stones and figures create a landscape of forests and mountains. They only need watering once every few weeks and are shade tolerant, so are fine even in a dark room. In a busy urban lifestyle, they offer a soothing presence."

Grazing animals and mountain climbing figures feature in these landscapes with depth. Gazing into them without too much thought will surely make you forget daily cares. You can make your own original versions (see page 78).

Sunlight is necessary for all living plants

You may be wanting to display greenery in a windowless room or a bathroom, but no plant can live completely without sunlight. Plants cannot photosynthesize with fluorescent lighting or an incandescent lamp. If you really want to enjoy greenery in a dark environment, try displaying objets such as dried flowers, wreaths, herbaria and so on. In the case of wreaths and herbaria, it's fun to use plants to create them to your own taste. Bring enjoyment to your life by using branches and leaves from pruned plants to display in the same way as cut flowers, or use them to form dried flower arrangements.

I started making these in 2010 as objets to complement plants. Ikebana arrangements, fruits and so on that have been dried are placed in jars, along with foliage, nuts and berries, seeds, roots and dried plants.

Various *objects d'art* using plants and flowers

For people who enjoy plants in all their forms, try incorporating preserved flowers and vegetation. Dried flowers can be hung as a bouquet on a wall, and it's also popular to make them into garlands or wreaths. Many arrangements include various types of herbs and are well suited to natural-style interiors. Herbaria are lovely, and need not be limited to ikebana—they can also be made using foliage, berries, nuts and so on. Combining favorite plants to make your own herbarium is part of their appeal. Additionally, seasonal plants such as Christmas wreaths, new year's decorations and so on should be incorporated into our daily lives.

Small flora and fauna motifs work well with greenery

When lining up smallish houseplants for display, try pairing them with knick-knacks and objets. If you're not sure what to match them with, items with natural motifs such as animals and minerals blend well with houseplants. It's fun to use the items to create forest scenery that calls to mind the environment in which plants grow. It's easy to combine houseplants with materials such as natural stones or shells along with different materials such as glass and iron. Posters and photos in frames, works of art and so on are also good choices. Consider how they contrast with the plants when creating the display.

ROUSSEAU

ROUSSEU made the series "A piece of nature" from parts of natural objects sandwiched between glass plates like specimens. The tranquil air of objets like these makes them a nice addition to a succulent or air plant display.

These geometric glass vases combine trapezoid forms. It's fun to display cuttings from the garden or potted plants in them. Wider or broader versions can also make great terrariums.

Hanging Your Plants

Even in a small space, display a lot of plants

Hanging pots are invaluable for displaying greenery stylishly. Plants can
be hung from hooks in the ceiling or from rails for curtains or lighting to
create a space with greenery. This means that large plants can be displayed
even in narrow areas and small rooms. Plants with trailing leaves are
perfect for hanging. Plants such as Rhipsalis and Hoya are often planted in
hanging pots in shops. Additionally, plants that are small but have a sense
of presence such as Platycerium bifurcatum (elkhorn fern; see page 72) can
completely change the look of a room.

Various methods for hanging

In order to be able to hang a plant, you can use a hanging pot that already has a hook, or a macramé or basket hanging made from hemp cord and so on. Use a planter that is light and has a drainage hole. In rental accommodation, people are reluctant to drill holes in the ceiling or walls. Hanging plants from the curtain rails is the easiest option, but if you want to hang them somewhere apart from by a window, a perforated board is a good option. Leaning the board against the wall will allow you to hang many plants from it. When watering hanging plants, take them outside and give them plenty of water. Leave them there until the water has drained out from the hole in the base, then return them to their original spots.

Hanging an Elkhorn Fern

No soil is required so they are easy to hang

Platycerium bifurcatum are a popular type of fern. They are better known as elkhorn ferns. The mysterious-looking ones, like the kind you see in Ghibli's animated movies, come under the scientific name of Platycerium. The elkhorn fern is a plant that grows as an epiphyte on trees and rocks, so in addition to its potted form, it can also be mounted onto kokedama, boards and driftwood. Those growing from kokedama are light, so are great for hanging. With their objet-like appearance, they work well as interior design items, and the large ones have such a presence that they could be symbol trees (see page 20). Elkhorn ferns attached to boards are covered on page 54 and page 80.

Using a Macramé Hanger

Just one plant hanger can brighten up a room

Combinations of knots form the patterns in macramé. In recent years, macramé plant hangers have become popular. We spoke to macramé artist Aki Hagino. "I first came across macramé in a vintage shop in California. I was fascinated by a beautiful macramé tapestry made in the seventies. Macramé has a strange charm in that it suits houses built a hundred years ago but also works in modern, sophisticated interiors. If you're going to use macramé hangings, I recommend plants with leaves that trail down such as Dischidia. Simply hanging it up will make the plant grow and grow, making a room more vibrant.

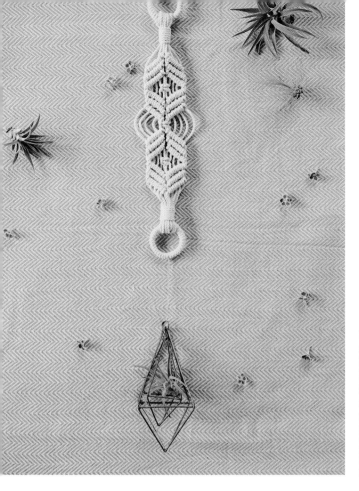

The delicate pattern is attractive in this macramé hanger that Aki Hagino has made. Hangings like this have the advantage of being able to maintain the flow of sun and air. Ms. Hagino says that the Dischidia hanging in her home has bloomed numerous times.

Ideal for hanging air plants

Air plants are perfectly suited to hanging. Hanging them keeps their leaves springier and helps them spread out further. It's also ideally suited to the characteristic tendency of air plants to molder in moisture. For those who don't want to go to the effort of removing the plant from the hanging each time they water it, a pot with no hole is a good option. If the pot has a hole, placing a dish underneath it inside the plant hanger will prevent it from dripping indoors. Simple macramé hangers can be made by hand. Why not enjoy teaming them with your favorite greenery?

Making a Succulent Group Planting

Materials
- container (with a hole in the base)
- mesh
- scissors
- tweezers
- wooden spatula
- wire
- trowel
- soil for succulents
- succulent seedlings

Place mesh over the hole in the container and fill container to about ⅓ with soil.

Prepare the seedling. Use the tweezers to lift them directly up and out of the pot. For large stock, gently loosen the soil by hand and separate plants. Leave soil on.

Arrange the succulents in your hand like a bouquet and place them in the container.

4

Once they look how you want them to look, use one hand to hold them in place while adding soil in from the side. Secure the seedlings firmly so they don't lift out of the ground.

5

Use the wooden spatula to press the soil down. Add soil until the seedlings are stable, repeating the tamping down of the soil. Add soil to app. ¼" (5 mm) below the edge of the container.

6

Use scissors to prune plants as desired and complete by adding seedlings, using U shaped wire to adjust their positioning and so on.

Complete!

(Editorial supervision: TOKIIRO. See page 189 for shop details)

Making a Moss Terrarium

Materials
- glass bottle (such as an apothecary bottle)
- moss (such as Leucobryum juniperoideum and Rhizogoniales)
- ornamental sand and stones
- syringe
- tweezers
- terrarium soil
- spray bottle
- miniature figures

1

Pour terrarium soil into the bottle. Add water until the soil is completely moistened and use the syringe to remove any excess.

2

Add ornamental sand or soil. Use scissors to cut the Leucobryum juniperoideum and use tweezers to plant it into the bottle a little at a time.

3

Take several Rhizogoniales seedlings, bundle them together and trim to the same size. Hold them vertically in the tweezers and insert into the soil.

4

Add in ornamental sand in different colors to create scenery. If the sand flows away, moisten it with water.

5

Use the spray bottle to rinse the entire area, then wipe the inside of the bottle with a tissue.

6

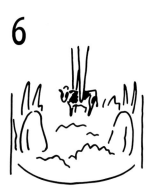

Use tweezers to position the figures and adjust the sand, stones and so on for overall balance to complete the terrarium.

Complete!

(Editorial supervision: Feel the Garden. See page 189 for shop details)

Mounting an Elkhorn Fern onto a Board

Materials
- Platycerium bifurcatum (if soil is attached, use a strong shower to rinse it off)
- transparent sewing machine thread
- scissors
- epiphyte board (here, we have used a special board. If using something such as a cedar board, drill holes in it or use nails to secure the plant)
- sphagnum moss
- potting soil (optional)
- fishing line (size 6)

1

2

After having soaked the sphagnum moss in water and wrung it out, place it on the epiphyte board in a donut configuration to form a base. If using soil, place moistened potting soil in the hollowed-out center.

Wind the sphagnum moss around the roots of the Platycerium bifurcatum. If there is soil on the roots, it may seep out whenever you water the plant, so make sure to rinse it off carefully.

3

Place the plant stock on the base and mold it into a round shape. The plant will develop nest leaves over the surface of the sphagnum moss. Once the composition is to your liking, pass fishing line through the holes to secure the plant to the board.

4

Fasten the plant stock to the epiphyte board with fishing line. If the board doesn't have holes, wind the line around hammered in nails. Make sure the fishing line doesn't pass over the growing tip.

5

Use clear sewing thread to secure sphagnum moss so it doesn't fall out. Pass it lightly over the top of the sphagnum moss, working from the board upwards to wrap the thread around in all directions. We recommend more than 15 rounds of wrapping. Lastly, cut the thread and pass the end into the sphagnum moss.

Complete!

(Editorial supervision: Flying. See page 189 for shop details)

Adding a Label to a Plant

Making a horticultural label by hand

Can you accurately name the houseplants in your home? Many of the plants that are known by their scientific names have quite difficult names, so write a label and attach it to the plant so you don't forget. In gardening, it is usual to add to the plant's name the date it was planted and other helpful horticultural information. If you search for "horticultural labels" or "gardening labels," you'll find various types such as those made from plastic or wood. Unlike outdoor flower beds exposed to wind and rain, indoor greenery can be labeled with a card, so it's possible to make the labels yourself. Why not try making some to complement your interior décor?

Hang the label from a branch or poke it into the soil. For a small cactus, use a fine, thin label for a clean look.

Use a label that pokes into the soil or a swing tag-type label depending on the plant.

Watering cans come in a fun range of sizes, colors and materials. The cans pictured here have a sliding lid that prevents water from spilling out. Choose your can to suit your needs, decor and personality. (cans from Royal Gardener's Club, manufactured by Takagi Co.)

Royal Gardener's Club <small>(All tools on these pages come from Royal Gardener's Club. See page 190 for shop details)</small>

Bottles that spray not only when the trigger is pressed but also when you release your finger are super convenient. For refreshing leaves and watering air plants, spray bottles are a must-have.

If you have a garden or balcony, you'll probably be using a hose regularly. A hose reel can help keep the hose neat and avoid kinks.

Choosing tools that reflect your personality is part of the fun of gardening. These trowels from the FIELD GOOD series come in colors named after flowers such as pink cosmos and white dandelion. (manufactured by Eizuka Works)

Some think of gardening scissors as large tools unsuited to small hands, but scissors that suit a small hand width are also available. Gardening scissors are invaluable for pruning. The pair above are made for ikebana.

Living with Greenery (1)

The atrium living room becomes an extra ordinary green space

At first sight, it's impossible not to admire Mr. Hamashima's home. Hanging plants fill the open atrium space of the living room, creating the atmosphere of a tropical rainforest. It's full of all kinds of plants, including Platycerium, Tillandsia (air plants) and caudex plants.

"We started living with plants when we built our house. The atrium creates an air of openness, so we try to make use of it to create an extraordinary space. Combining hanging plants and potted plants creates a space with an outdoor feel. The plants get their start when they come home with us. I think it's important to observe them every day, watch over their development as if they were our children and be fond of them, in order for them to live with us for a long time."

case study 1

Teru Hamashima

I'm a company employee living in Wakayama prefecture with my wife, children and two dogs in a compact standalone house with an atrium. I became interested in plants about five years ago and grow a wide variety including Platycerium, Tillandsia and caudex plants.

⊙ @botanical.0715

[1] The remarkable living room. The ceiling fan is on for the plants 365 days a year nonstop. [2] The garden trees at the Hamashima residence are beautiful, too! [3] Along with succulents, plant pots awaiting repotting line the shelves by a window. [Note: Mr. Hamashima often purchases items from the online store of TOKY (toky.jp) and targetplants in Osaka (targetplants.jp).]

4

[4] The collection on the stairs and the space beside them is a highlight. [5] A large pot in the kitchen. [6] From spring to fall, the plants are kept outside.

[7] The plants are gathered in the living room over winter. [8] An unusual caudex. [9] Tillandsia duratii, an epiphyte. [10] Focus on the combination of plants and pots. [11] There are several of the popular elkhorn ferns. Mr. Hamashima recommends the highly adaptable Bifurcatum for beginners.

Living with Greenery (2)

You can enjoy the garden of your dreams in an apartment!

For people who live in apartments but want gardens full of greenery, balcony gardening creator Ms. Rika can make their dreams take shape, creating spaces so overflowing with greenery that you would never guess they are part of an apartment.

"I started balcony gardening in 2007 when I moved into this apartment. It's a confined space, so there's a limit to the volume of plants that can be placed here. I created different height levels with wooden boxes and a fence, concealed the walls and floor and put bits and pieces up on display. I enjoy the entire space, not just the plants. I find healing in this lifestyle of touching the soil and cultivating plants and having a lot of greenery indoors. I'm living the life I dreamed about as a child, surrounded by plants."

1

[1] A workbench made by upcycling old materials. If an ornamental shelf isn't high enough, adjustments can be made with boxes and wooden planks. **[2]** Wood decking on the ground and timber and cloth concealing the wall make for a space with a lived-in feel.

case study 2

Ms. Rika

I want to convey the comfort of greenery and green spaces to as many people as possible, and I work as a balcony garden creator and as a coordinator at Midori no Zakkaya.

🄾 @skipkibun_rika

3

5

4

PART ONE: Creating a Life with More Greenery

[3] Group plantings can be enjoyed on balconies too. "I'm careful with cleaning up soil and dead leaves so as not to cause problems for the neighbors," says Ms. Rika. [4] Keep differences in height levels in mind when creating a space. [5] Greenery is teamed with bric-a-brac to decorate a sideboard. "Rather than placing items of similar colors or shapes together, I put different things next to each other to make it fun to look at." [6] The hanging is handmade macramé. Making it yourself means you can choose materials and designs to suit your taste.

7

[7] Use fake greenery in indoor spaces that don't get sunlight. **[8]** Sansevieria and Alocasia odora sit on a cabbage box to which casters have been added to make it easy to move around. **[9]** A coffee plant in a pot with an African pattern. Shifting plants to the balcony when climate permits is much healthier for the plant. **[10]** Pots and containers in various materials are fun.

8

9

10

Living with Greenery (3)

The atmosphere and balance are important

The light and shadow filtering in through lace curtains in Ms. Hana's living room is pretty. The well-placed greenery creates a comfortable space.

"The overall balance is important when displaying plants. I'm conscious of the overall atmosphere of the interior, so I create different height levels to prevent the positioning of the plants from becoming monotonous and team old furniture, posters, stools and other items together with the plants. When I use flowers and foliage at the dining table, I combine simple flowers with a quirky container or narrow the greenery down to one type for a balanced look. Sometimes I pick foliage from the olive or eucalypt trees or the rosemary or ivy in the garden for display. I'm careful about creating harmony with those, too."

case study 3

Ms. Hana

I'm housewife living in Saitama prefecture. I aspire to a life with a sense of atmosphere and am soothed by greenery every day. I enjoy living with plants and incorporate greenery into table arrangements and make wreaths and dried hanging bouquets for display.

[O] @h.m.m.150406

[1] Plants will grow quickly in the light-filled living room. The items surrounding the plants, such as the plant motif poster by the window and tin buckets, are attractive too.

[2] An acacia wreath evokes a sense of the seasons. **[3]** "If you're looking for items for your garden, head to an antique or thrift store! They have all kinds of things that will enhance the look of the plants, such as tin buckets, baskets and so on."

3

4

[4] Ms. Hana recommends Rhipsalis and Dischidia. Both types are tolerant to dryness and can be hung. The photo shows them after watering. [5] A basket makes a lovely outer pot. [6] A banana cake accompanied by an olive twig from the garden.

5

6

2

64 House Plants
You'll Want in Your Life

There are many ornamental plants in the world. Which ones will work in your life? We asked Ryusuke Sakaino, proprietor of plant shop AYANAS to carefully select some options. Here, we present each plant in an easy to understand way, from those with a contemporary vibe to more standard types.

How to Read the Plant Catalog

1 Scientific name

2 Family · Genus

3 Alternative names — If there are alternative names or names for distribution purposes they are listed here.

4 Common name — The name commonly used for the plant is listed here.

5 Cold tolerance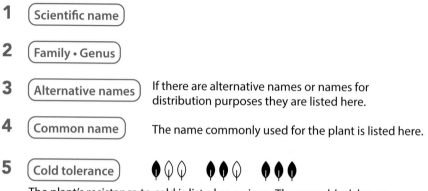

The plant's resistance to cold is listed as an icon. The more black leaves, the more tolerant of cold the plant is.

6 Size S M L

Shows the size of the individual plants published in this book. S indicates a small, table-top sized plant; M is a plant big enough that it needs two hands to hold it and L is a plant that needs to be placed on the ground. Even though individual plants might be small in photos, many of them grow big, so use this as a guide.

7 Watering type

A p177 **B** p177 **C** p178 **D** p178

Indicates the type of watering suited to the plant. The number beneath each item is the page number on which watering methods are explained.

8 Positioning

☀ outdoors 🏠 sunny indoor area 🏠 semi-shaded indoor area

The positioning suited to each plant is indicated with an icon. "Outdoors" is a garden or balcony; "sunny indoor area" is somewhere with a lot of sunlight such as next to a south-facing window; "semi-shaded indoor area" is somewhere that gets a few hours of sun each day or is just light enough to be able to read a newspaper.

Ficus elastica cv. 'Apollo'

A type of rubber tree (Ficus species). The Apollo is characterized by its undulating and shriveled leaves. It prefers sunny, well-ventilated places. However, if it is too sunny, the curled leaves won't open out properly, so place it in a spot that is on the bright side of shady. If it doesn't get quite enough light, the leaves will open out seeking sunlight. It is best placed by an east-facing window or slightly away from a south or west-facing window.

Key points

- Rubber trees in general are easy plants to grow
- If it is cold or there is insufficient sunlight, it may shed its leaves
- In winter, the room temperature next to a window drops, so take care.

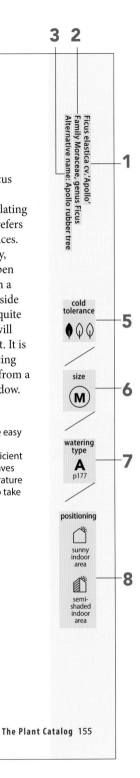

Ficus elastica cv. 'Apollo'
Family Moraceae, genus Ficus
Alternative name: Apollo rubber tree

1

cold tolerance

5

size

M

6

watering type

A
p177

7

positioning

sunny indoor area

semi-shaded indoor area

8

4 **3 2**

Agave potatorum 'Kisshoukan'

Agaves originate in the hot, arid regions of Mexico and Central America. Agave potatorum 'Kisshoukan' is one of the more popular varieties. Growth is slow, so it's a good choice for people who want to place a lot of small potted plants together.

Key points

- As it is a type of succulent, sun is important. Place it somewhere outdoors such as on a balcony.
- Overwatering or water collecting in a saucer placed beneath the pot will cause root rot, so exercise caution.

cold
tolerance

size

S

watering
type

A
p177

positioning

outdoors

The plant stock in the photo is the right size for a tabletop, but it grows to about a yard/ meter.

GREEN
LIFE

Aglaomorpha coronans

This fern has airy, sponge-like rhizomes. These roots are characterized by the way they creep over the ground, and when potted, they crawl over the container as if grabbing it. Although it is a fern, it is fairly resistant to dryness, but it grows best when it is kept sufficiently watered. It is native to hot, humid southeast Asia.

Key points
- Spray the leaves to keep them moist
- If kept indoors, it can easily become damaged from moldering, so make sure it has sufficient ventilation

The long fluttering leaves which look like they have serrations are a feature of this plant.

BOTANICAL

cold
tolerance

size

M

watering
type

A
p177

positioning

sunny
indoor
area

semi-
shaded
indoor
area

Asparagus macowanii

A member of the same family as the vegetable asparagus, this plant is not edible. It is characterized by its fluffy leaves, which are also used in cut flower arrangements. Apart from cold areas, if it is in a spot out of frost and the north wind, it can be left outdoors over winter. It would make a good accent for a balcony garden. Stock that has been trained with its roots exposed is rarely seen.

Key points
- Insufficient sunlight will make the plant grow spindly (long and gangly) so make sure it gets enough sun
- It is a fast grower, so make sure to repot, divide stock and prune regularly

cold
tolerance

size

M

watering
type

A
p177

positioning

outdoors

The fluffy leaves are a feature of this plant. It can grow up to 2 yards/meters tall.

Asplenium 'Cobra'

The intensely pleated, fleshy, rigid leaves of this foliage plant make an impression. As it makes such an impact, it's a great choice for high-profile places such as entranceways, living rooms and shops. It is in the same family as the bird's-nest ferns (Asplenium antiquum) which are often used as indoor plants in offices or public facilities. It tolerates shade, so can be kept in light shade or semi-shaded conditions.

Key points
- Works well in dark places and is a relatively easy variety to cultivate
- In seasons when ultraviolet light is strong, take care not to let the leaves burn under direct sunlight

cold
tolerance

size
L

watering
type
A
p177

positioning

sunny
indoor
area

semi-
shaded
indoor
area

A type of fern that grows in the tropics, it suits people looking for a unique potplant.

Aloe suprafoliata

An example of a fan-shaped aloe. If it only gets sunlight from one side, the leaves will start to rotate, so place it in a prime location with even exposure to the sun. It grows upright, with the trunk rising up like that of a tree. The plant stock gradually rises and fan-like leaves extend out from the tip of the trunk, creating a mysterious, attractive look. It originates from mountainous regions in South Africa.

Key points
- It is a small aloe, but can reach up to 12″ (30 cm) in diameter
- It likes sunlight and tolerates cold well, so except in cold areas can be kept even out on the balcony over winter

cold
tolerance

size

S

watering
type

A
p177

positioning

outdoors

sunny
indoor
area

FULL SUN

With its mysterious form like that of an unknown creature, this plant makes a big impact.

Aloe hybrid FLAMINGO

As the name suggests, the skin of this aloe has attractive pink-orange coloration like that of a flamingo. Throughout the year, it is a pinkish brown, but when it gets cold the entire plant turns a vibrant red to pink-orange color.

Key points
- It likes sunlight, so place it somewhere outside or by a window that gets direct sunlight
- It is a strong green color during warmer months

OUTDOORS

Plant stock that has changed color. The flower stem extends out from the center and has an adorable flower.

cold tolerance

size

S

watering type

A
p177

positioning

outdoors

sunny indoor area

Aloe antandroi

This small aloe has thin leaves that resemble rods. Although the plant looks delicate, it is quite sturdy. It branches out from where it is tried back (from where branches are cut off) so can be shaped into an attractive form through repeated pruning. It originates in Madagascar.

Key points
- An aloe is also a succulent and likes sunlight
- It is tolerant to cold, so apart from in cold regions, may be kept out on a balcony over winter

cold tolerance

size

watering type

A
p177

positioning

outdoors

sunny indoor area

Anthurium radicans

Anthuriums are known for their red, glossy, heart shaped leaves, but Anthurium radicans is the original species (it has not been altered through breeding). Deep creases mark the veins in the large, heavily trailing leaves. It is replete with the delightful foliage qualities of an "ornamental" plant. The flowers (bracts) resemble projections. This is a variety to be enjoyed for its dense foliage.

Key points

- It originates from tropical America and the West Indies. Particular care is needed over winter as it is vulnerable to cold
- It is susceptible to leaf burn, so make sure not to place it in direct sunlight in summer

cold
tolerance

size

(L)

watering
type

A
p177

positioning

sunny
indoor
area

semi-
shaded
indoor
area

Rhapis humilis cv. 'Unnann'

This variety has been popular in Japan since the Edo period. It has narrow leaves and a fresh appearance. As its name states, it originates from China's Yunan province. While it is associated with slightly older Japanese-style inns and public facilities and seems to have been around since the Showa era, once placed in a modern plant pot, it instantly looks contemporary. It tolerates shade well so works well in spaces with insufficient sunlight.

Key points

- It tolerates cold winters well and can survive winters even at temperatures of around 32°F/ 0°C
- It is highly tolerant of shade, but is sensitive to water loss, so if the soil dries out make sure to water it properly

cold
tolerance

size
M

watering
type
A
p177

positioning

sunny
indoor
area

This plant is defined by its vigorous, narrow leaves. Teamed with a modern pot, it can even take on a western appearance.

Licuala grandis

This palm has large leaves resembling a folding fan. It evokes the air of a tropical Asian resort. If it is placed in a sunny spot, the folds of the leaves will stand out and look magnificent. As it is shade resistant, it can be placed in bright shade.

Key points
- In its natural habitat, it grows in the shade of other plants, so keep it out of strong sunlight
- It is vulnerable to cold, so particular care is needed in winter

cold
tolerance

size

M

watering
type

A
p177

positioning

sunny
indoor
area

semi-
shaded
indoor
area

Aeschynanthus marmoratus

cold tolerance

size

(M)

watering type

A
p177

positioning

sunny indoor area

semi-shaded indoor area

While Aeschynanthus in general exude the exotic air typical of tropical plants, this variety is particularly noteworthy. The patterns spreading over its leaves make an impression, characterized by the different colors on each side of the leaves—they have green upper surfaces and purple undersides. The plant's appearance alters depending on where it is placed, allowing you to enjoy different looks. It is strong and robust, so is suitable for those just starting out with plants.

Key points

- As it is shade tolerant, it can be kept in semi-shade indoors. However, shade results in less pronounced patterns on the leaves, so we recommend keeping it somewhere sunny
- It likes well-ventilated spots, so can be hung up for display

Hanging

Aulax cancellata 'Bronze Haze'

A low growing evergreen tree from South Africa characterized by unique long, fine leaves. It has white feathery flowers from spring to summer. In the cold, the tips of the leaves turn a delightful bronze color, and if pruned, the branches last a long time as cut flowers that can be left to form a dried arrangement. Apart from in cold regions, it can be planted directly into the earth as a garden tree.

Key points

- Have 32°F/ 0°C as a benchmark of the degree of cold it can tolerate, and keep in a warm place over winter
- Use it as a garden tree or for greenery on a balcony

cold
tolerance

size

M

watering
type

A
p177

positioning

outdoors

OUTDOORS

Operculicarya decaryi

One of the popular caudexes (tuberous plants). It has gray bark and small, dense foliage and is often trained into the "exposed root" style (see page 28) to make use of the thick, winding roots which grow above the ground. Kept in a pot, the trunk does not tend to thicken, but in its native land of Madagascar, it can grow to a large tree with a thick trunk and a height of several yards/meters.

Key points

- Take care that it does not dry out over its growth period in summer
- It sheds its leaves and becomes dormant in winter, during which time it can be left somewhat dry

CODEX

Gasteraloe 'Green Ice'

This aloe-gasteria (a plant similar to an aloe) hybrid has blue-green leaves. The fleshy leaves are pointed at the tip and grow in layers, radiating outwards. It is known for its cool shades, so the name "Green Ice" is apt. This variety frequently puts out "pups" or new plant stock at its base.

Key points
- It is an extremely robust and easy to grow succulent
- Overwatering tends to cause root rot, so wait until the soil has dried out before watering

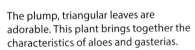
The plump, triangular leaves are adorable. This plant brings together the characteristics of aloes and gasterias.

cold
tolerance

size

(M)

watering
type

A
p177

positioning

outdoors

sunny
indoor
area

Calathea orbifolia

The large, airily soft leaves are the attraction of this plant. They are whitish green with green markings along the leaf veins. With its beautiful leaves, it lives up to the name "ornamental plant." As it originates in the dense jungles of South America, it does not cope well with strong sunlight in summer. It has a good tolerance for shade, so is fine placed away from a window in a room with bright shade (with enough light to read a newspaper).

Key points
- It loves high humidity so water the leaves and use a humidifier
- On the other hand, it has a tendency to develop root rot, so make sure it is in soil that drains well

cold
tolerance

size

M

watering
type

A
p177

positioning

sunny
indoor
area

semi-
shaded
indoor
area

Evocative of a tropical rainforest, the large leaves are perfect for interior decoration. It can also be displayed with small miscellaneous items.

Ficus microcarpa

This plant ranges in size from examples that fit in the palm of your hand to those large enough to reach the ceiling. It is a plant with many variations, with the standard form having exposed roots, and others having branches bent into shape or trained so that they cascade down past the edge of the pot. It adapts extremely well to its environment, growing completely differently depending on the amount of sunlight. In sunny spots, it has glossy, fleshy leaves that grow densely, while in shade its foliage is light, soft and a little more understated.

Key points

- It is a relatively easy to grow plant
- In winter, avoid placing it by a window or other places where the temperature drops

cold
tolerance

size

S

watering
type

A
p177

positioning

sunny
indoor
area

semi-
shaded
indoor
area

Echinocactus grusonii f. monst.

When you think of cacti, the long, tall, "column cactus" is what tends to come to mind, but this is a classic example of a "ball cactus" that grows in a globe shape. All kinds of variations have been created by varying spine length, thickness and color, and this is one of them. It has spine pads (the white areas at the base of the spines) that seem to be wearing hats, making for an adorable appearance. Its frequent forming of pups is another characteristic of this plant.

Key point

- Cacti tolerate dryness well, so beware of root rot caused by overwatering during winter and so on

cold
tolerance

size

S

watering
type

A
p177

positioning

outdoors

sunny
indoor
area

FULL SUN

Crassula undulata

A relative of the jade plant or "money tree," which has been known since ancient times for bringing wealth and good fortune. This variety features leaves with frill-like undulations. Its trunk thickens like that of a tree as it grows and the plant branches off. It has an appearance like that of a bonsai, and its distinctive qualities are enhanced with growth. This is a succulent that puts on a show when its leaves change color in cold weather. A "money tree" is an auspicious item, so is appreciated when given as a gift.

Key points

- Place it somewhere sunny with good ventilation. If indoors, next to a south-facing window is a good choice
- It is robust and easy to grow, so is suitable for greenery beginners too

cold
tolerance

size

S

watering
type

A
p177

positioning

outdoors

sunny
indoor
area

Cordyline fruticosa 'New Guinea Fan'

INTERIOR

This variety is harder to come by than many, but if you are looking for that unique item for an interior accent, this is for you. The purplish leaves reach up toward the sun and grow alternately on each side, forming a fan shape. As its name suggests, it is found in Oceania and southeast Asian countries such as New Guinea and Australia.

Key points

- If it does not receive sufficient sunlight, the leaves lose their color, so keep it indoors somewhere bright
- Water the leaves to prevent spider mite infestations

cold
tolerance

size

L

watering
type

A
p177

positioning

sunny
indoor
area

semi-
shaded
indoor
area

Sansevieria kirkii 'Silver Blue'

In recent years, a production system has become established so that kirkii 'Silver Blue' is more commonly seen. It is characterized by its rigid leaves with frill-like undulations. Like other Sansevieria, it is tolerant of dryness, and also copes well with shade so can be kept in places with little sun. The red edging along the leaves is adorable.

Key points

- Take care not to cause root rot through overwatering in winter.
  As a general rule, watering is not necessary from November to March in Tokyo
- It is shade tolerant, so can be kept in a place that does not get much sun

cold
tolerance

size

Ⓢ

watering
type

A
p177

positioning

sunny
indoor
area

semi-
shaded
indoor
area

Sansevieria hyb.
(gracilis × parva) 'kib wedge'

Sansevieria are robust and can withstand dryness, so could be said to suit beginners. They come in various forms, with 'kib wedge' featuring rod-shaped, narrow leaves. Many pups form at the ends of the runners that the plant puts out, making it a variety that can be trained to appear as if it is leaping out of the pot. It can be allowed to form clusters to fill the pot or can be divided to increase stock. It exudes a sense of vitality.

Key points
- Tolerant to dryness
- Take care not to cause root rot through overwatering in winter. As a general rule, once a month is adequate
- It is shade tolerant, so can be kept in a place that does not get much sun

cold tolerance

size
(S)

watering type
A
p177

positioning

sunny indoor area

semi-shaded indoor area

Sansevieria ehrenbergii 'Banana'

The 'Banana' is a small variety of Sansevieria ehrenbergii, which originates in Africa. The leaves are small and extremely thick and are characteristically curved exactly like bananas. Growth is slow and it can take more than a year to grow one leaf. It has some tolerance to shade, but making sure the whole plant gets plenty of sun is key for its growth. If only part of the plant receives sun, the leaves will tilt to one side and become spindly, meaning that the plant's characteristic shape will be lost.

Key points
- Take care not to cause root rot through overwatering in winter. As a general rule, once a month is adequate
- It is shade tolerant, so can be kept in a place that does not get much sun

cold
tolerance

size

S

watering
type

A
p177

positioning

sunny
indoor
area

semi-
shaded
indoor
area

Scindapsus pictus CV. Argyraeus

A variety in the Araceae family, which also includes other standard types of houseplant such as Pothos and Alocasia odora. The smooth, velvety, heart-shaped leaves have a soft gloss and silver mottling. The plant has a refreshing, cute appearance. It can be kept in shade, so is a good choice for entranceways and rooms where sunlight is not guaranteed. As it is a vigorous grower, even small seedlings that grace desks or spots in the kitchen will grow to overflow from their pots. It is the perfect choice for natural and Scandinavian-style interiors.

Key points

- Its leaves will burn under strong summer sunlight, so take care with its positioning
- It works as a hanging plant too
- It is susceptible to cold so take care with its positioning during winter

cold
tolerance

size

S

watering
type

A
p177

positioning

sunny
indoor
area

semi-
shaded
indoor
area

Schefflera elliptica

PARTIAL SHADE

A strong plant that is easy to cultivate, Schefflera is grown as a garden tree in warm regions. The widespread Hong Kong kapok species is found everywhere, such as in public facilities, offices, shops and home gardens. It is characterized by its glossy, oval leaves, but the elliptica's leaves are rounder and make a cute impression. The wider leaves reflect sunlight, bringing a sense of warmth to a room.

Key points

- Like the Hong Kong kapok, it is resilient to heat and cold so is easy to cultivate
- Dust tends to collect on the leaves, so make sure to wipe and mist them

cold tolerance

size

L

watering type

A
p177

positioning

sunny indoor area

semi-shaded indoor area

Syngonium podophyllum 'Neon'

Syngonium grows naturally in areas of Central and South America, such as Mexico and Costa Rica. It has many cultivars, including colored leaf varieties in vibrant shades of red, purple and silver. 'Neon' is a variety with attractive pale pink foliage that makes a slightly mysterious impression different from that of a flower. The mature, calm colors are attractive.

Key points

- It is a creeper, so is suitable for hanging
- Strong sunlight tends to cause leaf burn so take care with where the plant is placed over summer

cold
tolerance

size

M

watering
type

A
p177

positioning

sunny
indoor
area

semi-
shaded
indoor
area

Seidenfadenia mitrata

In its natural habitat, this variety of orchid attaches itself to trees. Even when it doesn't have flowers, its leaves that are the thickness of cooking chopsticks and its thick, white dangling roots make it quite a worthy sight that makes for an interior accent when hung on a wall or displayed as a hanging plant. The white flowers tinged with purple make a cute impression.

Key points

- Water every 3–4 days using a watering can to shower water over the entire plant stock
- Avoid cold places such as near windows over winter

cold
tolerance

size

M

watering
type

N/A

positioning

sunny
indoor
area

semi-
shaded
indoor
area

This plant is characterized by the fact that not only its roots, but also its leaves grow downwards. In its natural environment, it grows with its thick roots grabbing onto trees, rocks and so on.

Sophora microphylla

Tiny leaves form on the zigzagging branches of this plant in the Fabaceae family. Only the delicate seedlings are sold in stores, but if planted in the ground this plant can grow to a height of 2 yards/meters with thick branches. Although it seems delicate, it is a hardy plant. The branches will divide if trimmed, making for a plant with a more complex, interesting shape. Sophora Little Baby is a similar species but it is a different plant.

Key points
- Keep outdoors where it can get direct sunlight
- It copes well with the heat of summer and cold of winter but take care to protect it from frost and cold snaps

cold
tolerance

size

M

watering
type

A
p177

positioning

outdoors

Chamaedorea metallica

A small palm native to Mexico that grows large leaves at the ends of its outstretched branches. The leaves resemble arrow feathers and have a unique metallic sheen. As there is something singular about both the shape and color of the leaves, paired with the right pot, the plant can be a great interior accent. It is a slow, compact grower, reaching only about 19–28" (50–70 cm) in height, and can be displayed anywhere.

Key points

- As it is shade tolerant, it can be kept even in bright shade
- It is resistant to cold and is a relatively easy to grow variety

Chamaedorea metallica
Family Palmae, genus Chamaedorea
Alternative names: Chamaedorea tenella, Princess table palm

cold
tolerance

size

(M)

watering
type

A
p177

positioning

sunny
indoor
area

semi-
shaded
indoor
area

Cibotium barometz
Family Dicksoniaceae, genus Cibotium
Alternative names: golden wool, kinmouko,
golden chau chau

Cibotium barometz

This unique fern has rhizomes covered in brown animal-like fur that are soft to the touch. The bracken-like curled stems extend and put out leaves. In China it is an auspicious charm that brings good luck. While ferns are associated with shade, they also need sunlight. If they do not receive enough, the leaves will become twisted as they orient themselves in search of light from the sun.

Key points
- Grows well in places that receive only morning sunlight
- As it is a type of fern, make sure to water before the soil dries out completely

cold
tolerance

size

M

watering
type

A
p177

positioning

sunny
indoor
area

semi-
shaded
indoor
area

The fern-like green leaves sprout densely from the bushy rhizome.

BOTANICAL

Dischidia ruscifolia (million hearts)

Dischidia are vine plants. There are several varieties, and as its name suggests, the Million Hearts features dense, heart-shaped fleshy foliage. As it molders easily, place it somewhere with good ventilation. Plants in the Dischidia family are vulnerable to strong direct sunlight, but do like some sun, so will grow well-placed near an east-facing window.

Key points

- If kept indoors, they tend to become damaged from moldering due to insufficient ventilation, so watch for this
- Avoid direct sunlight in summer and keep somewhere bright and cool
- The main role of the roots is to attach to trees. Rather than watering the roots, boost moisture by watering the leaves

cold
tolerance

size

S

watering
type

A
p177

positioning

sunny
indoor
area

Dischidia nummularia variegata

cold
tolerance

size

(M)

watering
type

A
p177

positioning

sunny
indoor
area

A variety of Dischidia with a strong sense of vitality and an abundance of round leaves like counters in the game of Go. An epiphyte, in its native environment in the tropical regions of southeast Asia it grows by attaching itself to trees and so on. This quality can be maximized by mounting it onto items such as driftwood. Like other Dischidia, it likes bright, well-ventilated places.

Key points

- If kept indoors, they tend to become damaged from moldering due to insufficient ventilation, so watch for this
- Avoid direct sunlight in summer and keep somewhere bright and cool
- The main role of the roots is to attach to trees. Rather than watering the roots, boost moisture by watering the leaves

Dischidia formosana (Heart Jewelry)

Of the many Dischidia, Heart Jewelry is a relatively easy to cultivate variety, growing in both sunny and shady places. Just don't forget to make sure it is well-ventilated. Part of the round leaf is indented, giving it the heart shape from which its name derives. In spring, it has pretty white flowers like a lily of the valley. Like other Dischidia, it prefers bright, well-ventilated spots.

Key points
- If kept indoors, they tend to become damaged from moldering due to insufficient ventilation, so watch for this
- Avoid direct sunlight in summer and keep somewhere bright and cool

GREEN LIFE

cold
tolerance

size

M

watering
type

A
p177

positioning

sunny
indoor
area

Heart Jewelry makes a fresh, cute impression. It's perfect as a hanging plant.

Tillandsia capitata 'Mauve'

A type of Tillandsia (air plant) that has gray skin with a reddish tinge. The example in the photo is a miniature size, but it gets bigger as the plant puts out pups to form clusters (clumps). There are many varieties of Tillandsia available, so several different ones could be displayed together. As they do not require soil, they can be displayed in various ways as interior accents (see page 58).

Key points
- Use a spray bottle or the like to give them plenty of water, afterwards placing them somewhere where air circulates to prevent them from moldering
- See page 178 regarding watering

cold
tolerance

size

S

watering
type

C
p178

positioning

sunny
indoor
area

SUNNY PLACE

Tillandsia tectorum

Tillandsia (air plants) are covered with fine hairs called trichomes. Broadly speaking, they can be divided into "silver leaf types" which have an abundance of trichomes and "green leaf types" with sparse trichomes and a smooth texture, such as the bulbosa and butzii. The trichomes serve to diffuse strong sunlight and capture moisture in the air. "Silver leaf types" such as the tectorum are relatively resistant to dryness, making them easy to cultivate.

Key points
- When watering, use a watering can to shower the plants and make sure they get plenty of water, afterwards placing them somewhere where air circulates to prevent them from moldering
- See page 178 regarding watering

cold
tolerance

size

S

watering
type

C

p178

positioning

sunny
indoor
area

Dracaena Navi

The "tree of happiness" (Dracaena fragrans "Massangeana") is well known among the Dracaena. Even those who can't picture it are likely to have seen it, with its straight trunk and leaves protruding out like bamboo. The Navi is one of the less available, rarer types. It is stylish and closely resembles the Concinna, which is also in the Dracaena genus.

Key points

- Dracaena has been a standard plant for many years and is recommended for beginners as it is easy to cultivate
- It does not tolerate direct sunlight so take care with where it is placed

cold tolerance

size

Ⓛ

watering type

A
p177

positioning

sunny indoor area

semi-shaded indoor area

Dracaena burley

While it has the air of a plant in an old-fashioned café, depending on the pot and outer pot with which it is teamed, Dracaena burley works well in contemporary interiors. Its large, long, attractive mottled leaves make a striking impression and it works well as symbol greenery (see page 20) in living rooms, entrance ways, stores and so on. Its tolerance for shade makes it useful in a variety of situations.

Key point
- Dracaena has been a standard plant for many years and is recommended for beginners as it is easy to cultivate

PARTIAL SHADE

cold
tolerance

size

L

watering
type

A
p177

positioning

sunny
indoor
area

semi-
shaded
indoor
area

Dracaena hookeriana cv. 'Rothiana'

Also in the Dracaena genus, this variety is similar to the common Massangeana (tree of happiness) that is seen throughout Japan. Its leaves are more rigid and thicker than the Massangeana and are a monochrome pale green color. Its calm appearance makes it easy to incorporate as interior greenery. As it tolerates shade, it is recommended for areas where it is difficult to secure sunlight.

Key point

● Dracaena has been a standard plant for many years and is recommended for beginners as it is easy to cultivate

cold
tolerance

size

M

watering
type

A
p177

positioning

sunny
indoor
area

semi-
shaded
indoor
area

Thick leaves radiate out from the tall trunk.

Neoregelia Lila

With its leaves that grow in a rosette formation (radial formation) resembling a flower, the Neoregilia is one of the oldest, most popular houseplants. It comes in a range of colors, shapes and sizes including some expensive, rare varieties. There is a craze not only for cultivating and displaying them, but also for collecting them. This type of plant (tank bromeliad) can absorb water through its leaves, as water pools in the center of the leaf rosettes.

Key points

- Make sure to water so that water collects in the center of the leaves (see page 177)
- This plant is in the same pineapple family as the Tillandsia (air plant)

cold
tolerance

size

(M)

watering
type

B
p177

positioning

sunny
indoor
area

The vivid pink color makes an impression. Even small plant stock has an outstanding presence.

Pachypodium gracilius

The delicate branches growing from the plump, swollen tuberous base make for an adorable appearance, and this is a popular type of caudex. The thorny bark makes it hard to imagine, but the plant has pretty yellow flowers. It originates in Madagascar, where the arid, harsh environment has shaped its appearance. In winter it sheds its leaves and enters a period of dormancy.

Key points

- It has a tendency to develop root rot, so wait until the soil is completely dried out before watering. Watering is not necessary during the dormant period
- Some imported stock may not have roots yet, so check with the staff at the place of purchase

cold tolerance

size

(S)

watering type

A
p177

positioning

outdoors

sunny indoor area

CODEX

Once seen, this unique plant is not easily forgotten.
For many people, this is what comes to mind when they think of caudexes.

Pachypodium brevicaule

In Japan we call this tuberous plant (caudex) "Ebisu's smile." It is a variety of Pachypodium that grows by spreading out to the side like slime oozing. Leaves sprout here and there over the shapely plant stock, which has pretty yellow flowers. As it grows at high altitudes even in Madagascar, it is a little more susceptible to the heat of summer than other Pachypodium. In winter it sheds its leaves and enters a period of dormancy.

Key points

- It has a tendency to develop root rot, so wait until the soil is completely dried out before watering. Watering is not necessary during the dormant period
- Growth is extremely slow

cold
tolerance

size

S

watering
type

A
p177

positioning

outdoors

sunny
indoor
area

This plant stock can fit in one hand, but in its native habitat individual plants can grow to about a yard/meter.

Platycerium alcicorne var.Madagascar
Family Polypodiaceae, genus Platycerium
Alternative name: elkhorn fern

Platycerium alcicorne var.Madagascar

A type of Platycerium with deeply lobed sporophylls (sporangia-bearing leaves) that extend up in a wispy fashion. The circular reservoir leaves (leaves on the root side) have neatly formed veins and are very attractive. Both types of leaves are distinctive and make the strange impression of belonging to different plants. Board-mounted types are also available (see page 54, page 80).

Key points

- As it likes sun and good ventilation, it works well as a hanging plant
- See page 178 for how to water Platycerium

cold
tolerance

◆ ◇ ◇

size

M

watering
type

D
p178

positioning

sunny
indoor
area

Platycerium

The reservoir leaves spread out as if swallowing the terracotta pot.

Platycerium willinckii

This variety is characterized by the contrast of the completely upright reservoir leaves with the long, downward trailing sporophylls. If incorporating it into your interior design, the long, trailing sporophylls would be best showcased by being hung on a wall or suspended from a ceiling. Even one plant creates an interior accent, and even small plants will grow to a considerable size. They originate in the area around the island of Java, just below the equator.

Key point
- See page 178 for how to water Platycerium

With its somewhat birdlike form, it's understandable that this plant's Japanese name is "bat orchid."

cold
tolerance

size

(M)

watering
type

D
p178

positioning

sunny
indoor
area

Platycerium veitchii

Densely covered in stellate hairs (extremely fine, powderlike hairs), this Platycerium appears whitish all over. If placed in an area that receives good sunlight, it will reflect the sun's rays and appear completely white. Among the Platycerium with their lively, wild leaves, this variety makes a feminine, elegant impression. It works well not only in masculine interiors such as those with concrete walls, but also in regular rooms with white textured walls.

cold
tolerance

size

M

watering
type

D
p178

positioning

sunny
indoor
area

Key point

- See page 178 for how to water Platycerium

Hanging

A classic example of a soft, white Platycerium. The reservoir leaves are also a soft color.

Platycerium ridleyi

This Platycerium has distinctive reservoir leaves with creases that follow the lines of the leaf veins. In its native environment the reservoir leaves form balls which attach to grow on large trees. The sporophylls branch out finely as they grow and spread. In Japanese, "Platycerium" is written using the characters "deer antler fern," indicating a fern that resembles deer antlers. The magnificent sporophylls of the ridleyi truly represent Platycerium. If cultivated well, spoon-shaped sporangium will form.

Key point
- See page 178 for how to water Platycerium

The magnificent sporophylls have the impact of deer antlers.

Platycerium ridleyi
Family Polypodiaceae, genus Platycerium
Alternative name: elkhorn fern

cold
tolerance

size

M

watering
type

D
p178

positioning

sunny
indoor
area

Platycerium

Hydnophytum papuanum

This is an ant plant that grows as an epiphyte on trees in tropical regions. Out in nature, the plant has a symbiotic relationship with ants, which live inside the tuber and bring nutrients to the plant. The ants don't move indoors with the plant, however, leaving behind an empty maze of chambers where the ants once resided, and taking its nutrients from the potting soil instead. It is available as a potted plant, but as it grows naturally by attaching itself to trees, it can also be grown by attaching it to tree fern backing boards, kokedama and so on.

Key point

- It enters its dormant period in winter, so reduce the frequency of watering and move it to a warm place

cold tolerance

size
S

watering type
A
p177

positioning
sunny indoor area

Check out the round tuber! In its natural habitat, ants live in this section in a symbiotic relationship with the plant.

Ficus elastica cv.'Apollo'

A type of rubber tree (Ficus species). The Apollo is characterized by its undulating and shriveled leaves. It prefers sunny, well-ventilated places. However, if it is too sunny, the curled leaves won't open out properly, so place it in a spot that is on the bright side of shady. If it doesn't get quite enough light, the leaves will open out seeking sunlight. It is best placed by an east-facing window or slightly away from a south or west-facing window.

Key points

- Rubber trees in general are easy plants to grow
- If it is cold or there is insufficient sunlight, it may shed its leaves
- In winter, the room temperature next to a window drops, so take care.

Ficus elastica cv.'Apollo'
Family Moraceae, genus Ficus
Alternative name: Apollo rubber tree

cold
tolerance

size

M

watering
type

A
p177

positioning

sunny
indoor
area

semi-
shaded
indoor
area

Ficus elastica 'Jin'

cold
tolerance

size

(M)

watering
type

A
p177

positioning

sunny
indoor
area

A rubber tree with flecks (delicate spotted markings). The new leaves are light and gradually darken. The plant grows relatively quickly, and when the tree fills out the synergy of the leaf color and the look created by the markings makes it a symbol tree with a strong presence (see page 20). It is not often found, so if you happen to encounter one, have a go at growing it.

Key points
- Rubber trees in general are easy plants to grow
- If it is cold or there is insufficient sunlight, it may shed its leaves
- In winter, the room temperature next to a window drops, so take care.

Ficus triangularis

While there are as many as 800 types of Ficus, this rubber tree with inverse triangular leaves is one of the rarer ones. From far away, it appears normal, but up close, the shape of the leaves may come as a surprise. Place it somewhere that gets plenty of sun, such as near a south-facing window. Coincidentally, popular houseplants such as Ficus macrocarpa and Ficus benjamina are members of the Ficus genus, as is the fig tree with its delicious fruit.

Key points
- Rubber trees in general are easy plants to grow
- If it is cold or there is insufficient sunlight, it may shed its leaves
- In winter, the room temperature next to a window drops, so take care.

cold
tolerance

size

S

watering
type

A
p177

positioning

sunny
indoor
area

Ficus petiolaris
Family Moraceae, genus Ficus
Alternative name: red umbellata

Ficus petiolaris

A rubber tree with prominent red veins on its leaves, which are heart shaped like that of the Ficus umbellata. It also gets called "red umbellata." While the umbellata is popular, there is little stock of this type in distribution, so it is a good choice for people wanting a rubber tree that has something different about it. Seedlings (grown from seeds) swell into a ball-like shape at the base and are classified as tuberous plants, but those grown from cuttings do not thicken at the base.

Key points
- Rubber trees in general are easy plants to grow
- If it is cold or there is insufficient sunlight, it may shed its leaves
- In winter, the room temperature next to a window drops, so take care.

cold
tolerance

size

S

watering
type

A
p177

positioning

sunny
indoor
area

Ficus benghalensis

The benghalensis can be said to be a classic houseplant. It is a rubber tree defined by its large, oval leaves, which are a fresh green color with white veins. A vigorous grower, if left unattended it will get taller and taller. Make sure to cut it back regularly (pruning; see page 185) to circulate nutrients back to the base of the stock and thicken the trunk. It will branch out where it is cut, making for a fuller shaped tree.

Key points

- The large leaves tend to collect dust, so wipe them or rinse them off in the shower when watering
- If it is cold or there is insufficient sunlight, it may shed its leaves
- Many people choose this as their first pot plant as it is a variety that is easy to cultivate

BOTANICAL

cold tolerance

size

(L)

watering type

A
p177

positioning

sunny indoor area

A popular rubber tree. There are various shapes of tree around, so choose one to suit your taste.

Philodendron andreanum

There are many types of Philodendron, and it is a plant that looks completely different depending on the variety. The Andreanum features soft, smooth, lush, velvety leaves, which is why it is also called velvet kadsura (kadsura japonica). It is a houseplant with attractive leaf veins that are set off by the deep green of the leaves. Although it tolerates shade, placing it in a sunny spot is not only good for its growth, but allows you to clearly observe the texture of the foliage.

Key points

- It likes water, so take particular care that it doesn't dry out over summer. Watering the leaves is also effective
- It does not cope well with strong direct sunlight in summer, so take care with where it is placed

cold
tolerance

size

M

watering
type

A
p177

positioning

sunny
indoor
area

semi-
shaded
indoor
area

Philodendron grazielae

The Grazielae has adorable heart shaped leaves. The edges of the bright green leaves are curled back, creating a sense of solidity. Their fleshiness and gloss are also distinctive. During the plant's growth period in spring and summer, it grows vigorously and increases in volume, creating a bright, lively air. It has a relatively high tolerance for shade, so can be kept in bright shade (where there is enough light to read a newspaper). It is a plant that is easy to grow, even for beginners.

Key points

- It likes water, so take particular care that it doesn't dry out over summer. Watering the leaves is also effective
- Strong direct sunlight can cause leaf burn, so take care

cold
tolerance

size

S

watering
type

A
p177

positioning

sunny
indoor
area

semi-
shaded
indoor
area

Philodendron Tango

This variety has leaves similar to that of Philodendron kookaburra, which is a popular houseplant. The Kookaburra has an upright trunk, but this plant is a creeper. It is a vigorous grower and the vine and leaves spread in all directions, but can be kept in line by being trained onto a tree fern stake (a prop made from the trunk of a tree fern). Alternatively, if planted as a hanging plant, its rampaging form will create a decoration with a sense of volume and rhythm.

Key points
- It likes water, so take particular care that it doesn't dry out over summer. Watering the leaves is also effective
- Strong direct sunlight can cause leaf burn, so take care

cold
tolerance

size
(M)

watering
type
A
p177

positioning

sunny
indoor
area

semi-
shaded
indoor
area

Huperzia squarrosa

Hanging

An epiphytic fern with delicate, pointed, elm-like leaves that trail down gracefully. It branches out to increase stock. While it has a novel appearance, it is a plant to note as its popularity is increasing, following on from that of the Platycerium which is also a fern. It is a good choice for those wanting a plant that is "of the moment." As it is a fern, it does not cope well with drying out. Choose a place to hang it where it will be easy to water the plant and its leaves.

Key points

- See page 177 for points to note when watering ferns
- Place in semi-shade (somewhere that only gets a few hours of sun per day) for easy care

cold
tolerance

size

M

watering
type

A
p177

positioning

sunny
indoor
area

semi-
shaded
indoor
area

Philodendron billietiae

The large arrowhead shaped leaves and orange stems of this plant give it a unique form. There is a strong presence in even a single example of this plant, so it's recommended for people who want to have just one simple pot in the living room. Like other plants in the Araceae family, it is shade tolerant and is an easy variety to cultivate. It does not cope well with cold, so place it somewhere warm over winter.

Key points

- It likes water, so take particular care that it doesn't dry out over summer. Watering the leaves is also effective
- Strong direct sunlight can cause leaf burn, so take care

cold
tolerance

size

M

watering
type

A
p177

positioning

sunny
indoor
area

semi-
shaded
indoor
area

BOTANICAL

There is a beautiful contrast of green and orange in this pot. It's simple, yet looks fantastic.

Vriesea fosteriana 'Red Chestnut'

This ornamental plant has beautiful red-tinged leaves that radiate out (form rosettes). Its best angle is from directly overhead, so it is perfect for placing in low items of furniture (see page 51). Like the Neoregilia on page 147, it is a tank bromeliad and collects water at the center of its leaves.

Key points

- Make sure to water so that it collects in the center of the leaves (see page 177)
- Like the Tillandsia (air plant), it is in the pineapple family

cold
tolerance

size

M

watering
type

B
p177

positioning

sunny
indoor
area

Protea Juliet

An evergreen tree native to South Africa. The cut branches last a long time as a floral arrangement and can be left to form dried flowers. Apart from in cold regions, it can be planted into the ground as a garden tree. As it can tolerate temperatures down to minus 41°F/ 5°C it is fine if planted somewhere that is warm even in winter. It works well with olives, eucalyptus and wattles, and they can be planted together.

Key points

- It is cold-tolerant, so can be placed on a balcony or planted as a garden tree
- Its flowers are inflorescences or flower heads, meaning that many small flowers gathered together create the appearance of one flower

cold
tolerance

🌢🌢🌢

size

(M)

watering
type

A
p177

positioning

☼
outdoors

Heteropanax fragrans

It's a name you may not be familiar with, but this plant is closely related to the many varieties of Schefflera which are well known as houseplants (see page 133). It is often seen with its roots in the exposed root style, like Ficus macrocarpa (see page 28). The powerful roots are really something to see. From its appearance, it may look like a difficult plant, but it is quite normal in terms of care requirements.

Key point
● It is quite a fast grower, and is a variety that is satisfying to cultivate. Enjoy pruning and repotting it too (see from page 182)

cold
tolerance

size

M

watering
type

A
p177

positioning

sunny
indoor
area

semi-
shaded
indoor
area

The eye tends to be drawn to the spectacular roots, but the glossy shine of the leaves is also distinctive.

PLANT

Bombax ellipticum

This caudex plant has the trait of storing water in its base to protect itself from drying out. Pruning the branches and the trunk directs nutrients and moisture back to the base, making it thick and plump. Repeating this process over many years results in the formation of a rounded base. In winter, the plant sheds its leaves and becomes dormant. The shaved head look of the tree is emphasized by the thick trunk, giving it a strange appearance like an art object.

Key points

- It is a variety that you can enjoy shaping in the same way as a bonsai
- Once it has shed its leaves, reduce the frequency of watering and let it dry out a bit

cold
tolerance

size

M

watering
type

A
p177

positioning

outdoors

sunny
indoor
area

CODEX

The thickened root base. The cracked texture of the bark on the trunk is a feature of age.

Mimetes cucullatus Crackerjack red

An evergreen tree native to Australia and South Africa. It is similar to a Leucaendron, but the leaves are shorter and more defined. The red leaf tips make for an attractive appearance. Other than in cold regions, it can be planted into the ground as a garden tree. As it can tolerate temperatures down to 32°F/ 0°C it is fine if planted somewhere that is warm even in winter. Similarly to the Protea Juliet on page 166, it is popular as a cut flower and in dried flower arrangements.

Key points

- It tolerates cold, so can be placed on a balcony or grown as a garden tree
- It works well with plants that make a wild impression such as Agave (page 110) and cacti

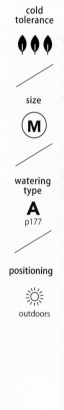

cold
tolerance

◆ ◆ ◆

size

(M)

watering
type

A
p177

positioning

☼
outdoors

Euphorbia 'Sotetsukirin'

This succulent is like a miniature version of the sago palm (Cycas revoluta) that is often encountered as a garden tree. It is the result of crossing the Euphorbia Kaimagyoku, which is itself a hybrid of Euphorbia bupleurifolia and Euphorbia mammillaris, with its original parent, Euphorbia bupleurifolia. It often puts out pups, so is a variety that is satisfying to cultivate. It lignifies (hardens in the way that a tree does) little by little as it grows, creating a cool look that is full of character.

Key points
- It likes sun, so place it on the balcony or outside
- It does not cope well with cold, so keep it somewhere inside that gets sun in winter

cold
tolerance

size

S

watering
type

A
p177

positioning

outdoors

Yucca rostrata

Since the start of the 00s, Rostrata has come to be widely seen in outdoor plantings and landscaping of private homes where the climate is compatible. The types with long, freestanding trunks and those with trunks that branch out are particularly popular. It is sometimes seen planted in dry gardens (gardens that bring together plants that are resilient to dryness) with succulents, cacti and Australian plants. Growth is slow, so it is useful for areas where you don't want the look of the plantings to alter much.

Key points
- It copes well with cold and can grow to several yards/meters outdoors
- It tolerates drying out well, so is a plant that doesn't need much effort

cold
tolerance

size

M

watering
type

A
p177

positioning

outdoors

Rex Begonia

When it comes to rhizomatous begonia, there is a wide variety of colors, patterns, textures, shapes and sizes. In the begonia world, enthusiasts trade rare types among themselves. Types that were created by hybridizing the original Begonia Rex type are widely distributed under the name Rex Begonia. Of the types that are generally available, many are inexpensive, so it would be interesting to put a collection together.

Key points
- It hates strong summer sun, so keep it in bright shade (with enough light to read a newspaper)
- It likes humidity, but make sure that the soil drains well

cold
tolerance

size

M

watering
type

A
p177

positioning

sunny
indoor
area

semi-
shaded
indoor
area

Ledebouria socialis 'Violacea'

When we think of bulbs, we tend to think of plants such as tulips and hyacinths, but this is a bulbous succulent—a succulent that forms a bulb. This variety is distinguished by the attractive leopard print spreading over the leaves. Coming from a plant with such a quirky appearance, it's hard to imagine, but it has cute flowers like a lily of the valley. When it sheds its leaves in the cold, the purple-skinned bulb appears. It's a plant with more to it than flowers.

Key points
- Flowers bloom from spring to early summer
- When it sheds its leaves and enters its dormant period, it can be kept on the dry side

cold
tolerance

size

M

watering
type

A
p177

positioning

outdoors

sunny
indoor
area

3

Some Things You Need to Know

Whenever you find a plant you like, it dies straight away.
Or you're not sure why, but your plant is just not thriving,
or maybe it was a good shape when you bought it but now it
won't grow the way you want it to….
This section covers the basics for solving issues such as these.
Plants are living creatures, so for a long life together, get to
know the basics for their care.

Watering Basics

Modulation of watering is important

Water is important for plants. If they don't have it, they will die, but if they are constantly soaked in water the roots become unable to breathe and will weaken. It is said that the most common cause of death for potted houseplants is root rot caused by overwatering. Wait until the soil has dried out until watering. The degree of dryness in the soil will vary depending on the size of the plant, its characteristics, its location and so on. If you touch the soil and it is smooth, that is a sign that it is OK, so give the plant plenty of water until it is running out of the base of the pot. Picture the water in the pot as being refilled and repeat two or three times for thorough watering. If you give the plant a little water every day, the old water will collect in the pot and may lead to odor or root rot. Wait until the soil has completely dried out before watering again. If the pot is of a size that allows it to be moved, shift it outside, to the kitchen, bathroom or some other "easy drainage" place when watering. Showering the entire plant, leaves, branches and all, will also rinse off any dust. Once water stops running out from the bottom of the pot, return it to its saucer or outer pot. If water collects in the saucer, empty it out, as it will lead to odor and mold.

Carry out seasonal adjustments and leaf watering properly too

In winter, gradually reduce the frequency of watering. Plants' growth slows and they don't require much water, so leave them on the dry side. Conversely, in summer, they take in a lot of water and dry out easily, so take care to keep up with the watering. Additionally, in seasons with high temperatures or high humidity, plants tend to molder if left indoors in a closed room after watering, so make sure that air is circulating where they are placed. Leaf watering means to water the leaves directly, using a spray bottle or something similar. This is particularly effective in residential environments that have a tendency to be too dry. Too much leaf watering doesn't generally cause problems. Leaf watering also helps deter pests such as spider mites. Try to make an active effort to water the leaves.

Watering According to Plant Type

The basics of watering were covered on the previous page, but there is a knack to watering depending on the type of plant. In this book, we have broadly divided plants into four types to cover watering know-how. These types correspond to the watering types listed in the plant catalog in Part 2.

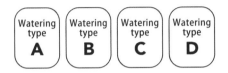

Regular type

Most plants can be watered using the basic method discussed on the previous pages. However, ferns do not cope with dryness, so water them before the soil dries out completely. They like the soil to be moist. Carry out leaf watering regularly too. Furthermore, if plants are kept outside, you'll need to take care during summer. Even if the soil is not dry in the morning, the high daytime temperatures can quickly dry it out. Placing plants somewhere that gets morning sun but becomes shady in the afternoon prevents the soil from sudden dryness.

Tank Bromeliad type

Tank bromeliads belong to the Bromeliad family (pineapple family). Neoregelia, Vriesea, Hohenbergia and other such plants are tank bromeliads. Their major characteristic is their ability to absorb water and nutrients not only through their roots, but through their leaves as well. Watering onto the soil is the same as for other types, but they should also be watered so that water collects in the conical section formed in the center where the leaves overlap. Showering the plant with a watering can and letting water overflow from the conical part of the plant means that the soil gets watered at the same time. Make sure to check whether the water in the conical section is depleting. If it is left for a while, the water may start to turn putrid and smell, so tilt the pot to pour out the old water and pour new water in to replace it.

Tillandsia type

This includes air plants that grow as epiphytes on rocks and trees. As they are not planted in soil, people tend to think they don't need watering, but it is of course necessary. Use the shower from a watering can or spray bottle to water the entire plant stock until it is dripping wet. After watering, make sure the plant is in a well-ventilated spot to prevent damage from moldering. Water 2–3 times a week from spring to fall, and about once a week in winter. In summer, watering during the day may cause damage from moldering, so do it in a cool spot from the evening onwards. For plants such as the Tillandsia xerographica which is structured to collect water in its leaves, hang it upside down to let water run out. Furthermore, silver leaf type tillandsias which are covered in white hairs (trichomes), such as the Tillandsia tectorum, are relatively resilient to dryness, so adjust their watering accordingly.

Platycerium type

Most plants of this type originate from tropical regions. Their major characteristic is their upward growing sporophylls and reservoir leaves which cover the base of the plant (see page 150). Make sure that water reaches the back of the reservoir leaves (inner side). Too much water will cause the reservoir leaves to die and discolor. If planted in a pot, aim to water once every 1–3 days from spring to fall and 3–4 times a month in winter, using a watering can to shower plenty of water over the entire plant stock. If the plant is covering the pot, fill a bucket with water and soak the entire pot in it. Plants mounted on boards or into kokedama tend to dry out, so take care to water the board or the kokedama properly. Small seedlings have a tendency to dry out, so water their leaves regularly.

Daily Care to Prevent Plants from Dying

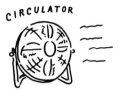

Don't close windows—let air circulate

In order to prevent plants from dying, good ventilation is necessary. For transpiration, one of the plant's processes, to occur, air circulation is invaluable. Inadequate ventilation may cause pest infestations to occur and mold to grow on the soil. Ideally, place plants somewhere well-ventilated where they can receive a natural breeze. If they are shut indoors while you are out, create air flow with an air circulator or fan. If your living environment permits it, installing a ceiling fan is also a good idea. However, don't allow the plant to come in direct contact with strong winds from air conditioning or fans. The leaves and stock will get extremely dry, which is hard on the plant. Instead, make sure the plant is getting gentle breezes from various directions.

Check on them often

If you're trying to grow healthy plants but they end up dying, start by making sure to check on them every day. By observing them daily to see whether the soil or leaves have dried out, if insects are settling in, if an indoor plant is getting good sunlight and ventilation, whether the leaves are becoming discolored and so on, you'll be able to notice even small changes, and if problems arise, to identify the cause and take appropriate action. Rather than thinking of it as having to look after plants every day, try greeting them in the way you would greet your family every morning and check on their condition. You might also make happy discoveries such as new shoots and buds.

What Kind of Environments Do Plants Like?

Creating as warm and humid an environment as possible

When plants are being cultivated, they may be subjected to weather damage, withering and dying from summer heat, shedding leaves from being unable to cope over winter, having branches broken due to storms and so on. We will cover points to note about extreme weather conditions such as heat and cold in the next pages, but what is the best environment for plants to begin with? Firstly, as mentioned previously, they need good sunlight and ventilation. They also need warmth and humidity. Climates similar to that of the rainy season are ideal for houseplants that grow in tropical regions. Choosing plants compatible to your climate and environment will result in plants growing vigorously and healthily.

Points to note in summer

In summer, plants may wither from insufficient watering, molder from the heat, become infested with spider mites or become damaged from leaf burn due to ultraviolet rays. It is a season in which they damage easily, rather than actually dying. In a closed room in summer, plants will dry out from the high temperatures. This is the type of conditions that spider mites like, so ensure the room is well-ventilated and water leaves to prevent infestations. Additionally, avoid exposing plants directly to the breeze from an air conditioner as it can cause dehydration and lead to discoloration of the leaves. Find a place for plants that gets the gentle light from dawn through to mid-morning but is shaded during the hours of the day when the sun's rays are strongest. Incidentally, it seems that many professionals and people who are experienced at cultivating ornamental plants keep them outside during their growing season, such as on a balcony, apart from in winter. They move them indoors when a typhoon is predicted, or for tall potted plants, lean them up against a wall to prevent the wind from breaking their branches or lie them on their sides and secure them with weights. There is no problem with plants receiving heavy rain. When strong winds are a concern, take measures as you would for a typhoon.

Points to note in winter

Dry, cold winters are highly stressful for plants which like warm, humid conditions. It is a time when plants are prone to root rot caused by overwatering, frost damage from the cold, discoloration due to dryness and deterioration of condition from lack of ventilation in a sealed space. Bring plants that are susceptible to cold indoors. Apart from in cold regions, some plants can winter outdoors, but bring them inside if there is a cold snap. As a rule, many plants can survive winter at temperatures down to 41°F/ 5°C. Just as in summer, make sure they don't receive air directly from a heating unit. Use a spray bottle to water their leaves as a measure against dryness in conjunction with a humidifier. Additionally, place them somewhere that is warmed by a heater due to it being frequented by members of the household. Windowsides get cold, so place only cold resistant succulents or cacti there. If it seems that they would receive enough light indoors, plants can be moved into sunlight during the day and moved back to somewhere that doesn't get cold at night. If there are too many plants for this to be practical, move them around on a rotating schedule or rearrange things to make it easier to care for them indoors.

When you're away

Have your plants ever died over the summer holidays or other times when you were away for a while? This was due to damage from heat and moldering that is brought on by high indoor temperatures and a lack of ventilation. Do some advance preparation if you are going away. For absences of 3–4 days, if you water as usual, the pot should retain enough water. Positioning is more important than watering. Somewhere outdoors with shade (on the north side or in the shade of something such as a fence) and good air circulation is best. On an apartment balcony, be careful of the hot air from next door's air conditioning unit outlet. A cool spot out of direct sun with shade and good air flow is ideal.

For ferns, if they are potted, place them in a tray of water ¼–1" (1–2 cm) deep. For long absences of 2–4 weeks, it would be good to ask friends or neighbors to water plants. Explain the frequency of watering, such as once every 4–5 days, before you leave. If it is difficult to ask someone else to care for your plants, there are products available that can be set to water automatically. They can be purchased at home centers, gardening stores, over the internet and so on. Make sure to give plants plenty of water when you get back home.

Fertilizing Your Plants

Other than watering and exposure to the sun, fertilizer is the other source of nutrition for plants. There are different types of fertilizer, with organic fertilizers derived from natural sources and chemical fertilizers made from synthetic ingredients. Organic fertilizers are made from ingredients such as oil cake and bone meal and take effect slowly, so you are less likely to experience problems with them, however their strong odor is a disadvantage. Artificially produced chemical fertilizers don't smell and are suitable for plants cultivated indoors, but if plants are given too much it can cause the roots to burn, so care is needed. In terms of timing, fertilizer can be given during the plants' growth period from around April to September. There are two types of fertilizer: slow-release basal fertilizer and quick-release supplemental fertilizer. Basal fertilizer is used by mixing it into the soil when planting or repotting so it will remain effective over a long period. Supplemental fertilizer is used to replenish insufficient nutrients during growth. There are quick-release liquid fertilizers and slow-release fertilizer pellets. The liquid type can be given during watering. Dilute it to the concentration indicated to use it. Fertilizer pellets are a solid type of fertilizer that are strewn over the soil surface and work slowly and continuously. Depending on the plant, it may prefer poor soil and not require fertilizing, so make sure to use fertilizer in accordance with the plant's characteristics.

Repotting Basics

What happens if plants are not repotted?

The root section of a plant is important. Most plants absorb nutrients and moisture from the soil through their roots in order to grow. In a potted plant, there is a limited amount of soil, and once the nutrients are gone, it is difficult for the plant to grow purely from the nutrients in water. On top of this, in the limited space inside the pot, the growing roots are crowded and have nowhere to go. This results in the roots becoming clogged and it becomes necessary to repot. If you don't repot the plant, the roots will stop the soil from absorbing water, more frequent watering will be necessary and growth will slow. Change the soil, use a bigger pot and remove old soil and excess rootstock to keep the roots in shape.

How do I know when to repot?

As the roots are inside the pot, they are not visible. However, roots mounting up on the soil surface or roots becoming exposed or emerging from the hole in the base of the pot indicate that it's time to repot. Additionally, if you notice that the ends of the leaves are withering or new shoots are not growing well, consider repotting. The roots may be crowded inside the pot. When repotting, the roots inevitably incur some damage, so do it just before the plant's growth period. Even if the plant is damaged, if it starts to grow afterwards, it will soon recover. If a plant is healthy and you don't want it to grow large, there is no need for repotting.

How do I repot a plant?

Repotting is not difficult. You will need new potting soil, a pot of the right size for repotting, mesh for the base of the pot, stones for the base of the pot, scissors and disposable chopsticks or cooking chopsticks. In terms of the size for the new pot, let's say you have two potted rubber trees, both in size 5 pots. One has roots that have grown so much that they are clogging up the pot, so it is necessary to plant it into about a size 8 pot. The roots of the other rubber tree, though, haven't extended out much so a size 6–7 pot might be fine. It's not necessarily the case that you'll need the next pot size up when repotting, so check the condition of the roots to select the right pot.

Once you've prepared the necessary items, remove the plant from the pot. In order not to damage the roots, don't break off soil from around them (the root ball) but put the plant as-is into the new pot and cover it with soil to finish off. This raises the question of why you don't brush off soil or cut off roots. The reason is that it is fine to use scissors to cut off old roots (the ones that have gone brown and are hollow inside), but if you don't know which are the old roots, repot the plant as-is. If you cut off healthy roots it will affect the plant stock, so until you have some experience, leaving things as they are is safer. Once you can judge the condition of the roots, have a go at repotting for real.

Repotting Step by Step

You will need
- potting mix
- a replacement pot (larger than the current one)
- mesh for the pot base
- stones for the pot base
- disposable chopsticks, a wooden stirring stick or cooking chopsticks

1

Carefully remove the plant from the pot, leaving the roots intact. If it is hard to remove, lightly tap the side of the pot while pulling it out.

2

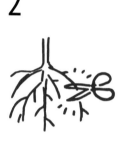

Lightly brush off soil and roots, and neaten up old roots if necessary. If you're not experienced, it's fine to leave things as they are.

3

Place mesh and stones at the base of the replacement pot to improve drainage. Akadama soil can be used in place of stones.

4

Pour in soil, checking the height of the soil to add the plant in and make adjustments.

5

Add soil, pushing a chopstick in between the root ball (soil around the roots) and the pot and filling up any gaps between roots with soil so that it is evenly distributed.

6

Give the plant enough water so that it trickles out from the base of the pot. Keep the plant out of direct sunlight and in bright shade for about a week.

Maintaining a Plant's Shape

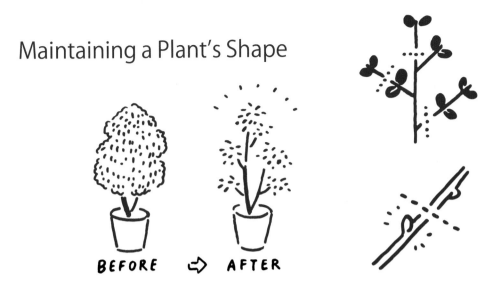

BEFORE ⇨ **AFTER**

Prune to adjust the form

Plants are growing every day, producing more leaves, branches and buds. As more leaves form and branches get longer, the plant's shape alters. Once it gets dense, prune off excess branches and leaves that are hampering growth. You may feel reluctant to cut off leaves and branches that are growing so well, but pruning actually encourages new buds to emerge and has the advantage of stimulating growth, so don't hesitate to do it. The best time to prune is during the growth period from April to July. Pruning neatens the shape of the plant and improves air flow. After pruning, place the plant in a sunny spot to facilitate budding.

Reduce the number of buds to consider overall balance

Pruning is not about blindly cutting off branches and leaves. The key points are to reduce the number of buds, cut off branches to prevent crowding and create overall balance in the shape of the plant. Cut at a point above the bud. This will allow the next bud to grow smoothly. As regards branches, the more they branch out the more nutrients become dispersed, leading to shabby branches and poor air circulation. Therefore, once branches divide three or four times, cut them back to their second point of division. If there is an overall imbalance of branches, trim off the ones that are sticking out to neaten the form of the plant. If pruning is done all at once, it will put strain on the plant, so take it one step at a time and see how things go.

Q&A About Common Plant Problems

  The plant in the entranceway isn't looking very healthy. I have the light on and the air circulates well, so what is the problem?

  Every plant needs sunlight. The brightness of the light is meaningless.

Plants are essentially grown outdoors. You may think that switching on a light makes it bright, but the brightness of a light has no meaning for a plant. It won't die immediately, but it will gradually lose its vigor. Place it somewhere where it can receive bright sunlight.

 Is it alright to choose plants based on my taste alone?

It is also important that they are suitable for where they will be placed.

It's easy to become fond of a plant you've fallen in love with at first sight and feel motivated to properly care for it. But if it is a variety that isn't suited to the environment in which it is placed, it may die. Communicate with the staff when purchasing the plant about where you plan to keep it to find out whether it is a good environment for the plant. The plant catalog in this book also lists suitable places for plants, so use it as a reference.

 I watered my plant because it didn't look well, but now it looks even worse…

Not looking well doesn't necessarily mean a lack of water.

Sometimes it may be the case that water is insufficient, but conversely, being overwatered is also a possible cause. Apart from that, lack of sunlight, poor ventilation and other reasons may be considered. Think about whether the plant is suitably positioned. If it is overwatered, stop watering for a while, move it somewhere with good ventilation and sunlight and see what happens.

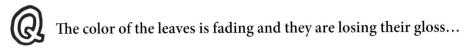 **The color of the leaves is fading and they are losing their gloss...**

 This may be caused by spider mites. Get rid of them.

If leaves are becoming speckled with white, feel rough and are losing their gloss, spider mites may be the reason. They can easily spread to other plants, so get rid of them quickly. Rinse the entire stock thoroughly in the shower. Prevent spider mites by placing the plant somewhere with good air circulation and water the leaves (see page 176).

 There are small flies flying around the plant...

Watch out for overly moist soil or water in the pot saucer.

Small flies may be attracted to damp earth or water remaining in the pot saucer. They tend to appear when fallen leaves accumulate and when organic fertilizer is used. Remove fallen leaves and don't allow water to collect in the pot saucer. Check inside the outer pot as well, and use chemical fertilizer. Remove an inch or so (a few centimeters) from the surface layer of soil and replace it with akadama soil. Mulching (covering the surface) with pebbles and so on is also effective. Try killing the flies with a gentle insecticide such as a solution of water and peroxide.

 The plant has got thin and gangly and looks shabby...

It is lacking sunlight. Place it somewhere sunny.

Fading leaf and stem color, widening gaps between leaves, extremely large leaves and spindly growth are due to a lack of sunlight. Sunlight reaching indoors by itself tends to be inadequate. Reconsider where the plant is placed and gradually move it to a brighter spot that gets plenty of sun.

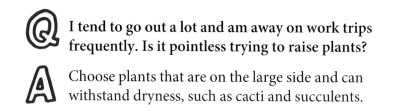 **I tend to go out a lot and am away on work trips frequently. Is it pointless trying to raise plants?**

A Choose plants that are on the large side and can withstand dryness, such as cacti and succulents.

Choose plants that are resilient against dryness and plant them in large pots that can hold a lot of soil. This allows you to reduce the frequency of watering. In the case of a 3–4 day absence, give plants plenty of water and place them outside in a shaded area where air circulates well, and the pot will retain its moisture. If you are worried about being too busy to care for plants, choose types that cope well with dryness from the plant catalog in this book.

 **The leaves and branches are growing in a lopsided way and the shape of the plant has changed.**

A Plants search for sunlight as they grow.

If a plant is placed on a sunny windowsill, it will grow in the direction of the light that it is trying to absorb. The reason for this is that plant hormones stimulate growth on the shaded side. Change the orientation of the pot occasionally so that the entire plant receives sunlight.

Credits

Ayanas Botanical Works

"Ayanas" means to form beautiful patterns and scenery from a collection of colors and shapes. Ayanas offers plants that will bring color to your life. Based in Takasaki City, Gunma prefecture, Ayanas is a boutique ornamental plant store as well as designing external structures, plantings and exteriors.

URL : ayanas.jp   @ayanas.jp

TOKIIRO

TOKIIRO is Yoshinobu Kondo, a horticultural designer specializing in arrangements made from succulents. Through diverse activities including green design, garden design and facilitating workshops, he creates stories (arrangements) that live in spaces (containers). He is co-author of *Stylish Succulents* (Tuttle Publishing, published in Japan as *Tanikushokubutsu Seikatsu No Susume* by Shufu-to-Seikatsusha).

URL : www.tokiiro.com   @ateliertokiiro

Feel The Garden Moss Terrariums

Feel the Garden produces and sells greenery, with a focus on moss terrariums. Their popular monthly workshops allow people at each level from beginner through to advanced to experience creating terrariums. If you are in Japan and would like details or reservations, please visit the website.

URL : www.feelthegarden.com   @feelthegarden

Flying (Flying Ltd.)

Flying designs spaces, displays for commercial facilities and so on. In addition to producing and selling epiphyte boards for Platycerium (elkhorn ferns), from spring to fall they offer epiphyte board usage workshops on an irregular basis. Their epiphyte boards are available at https://imamanet.stores.jp/, with custom orders possible for boards of different sizes and shapes.

URL : https://imama-net.stores.jp/   @flying_design

SNARK Inc.

An architecture design firm based in Gunma and Tokyo. Their diverse activities include designing furniture and other products; interior design; planning, design, and construction management for new housing and public facilities as well as event planning and management. For inquiries about the steel product series published in this book, contact press@snark.cc

URL : www.snark.cc   @snark_inc

aarde

A specialist pot plant and planter mail order store created for the general public by Oumi Toki, a long-established wholesaler specializing in plant pots for nearly 70 years and handling more than 2500 types of plant pot at any given time.

URL : www.aarde-pot.com

HACHILABO

HACHILABO works on the concept that the plant (leading role) and plant pot (supporting role) have a symbiotic relationship, with each drawing out the other's unique traits. Far from being bland, they are "outstanding support actors" with their own unique characters.

URL : www.8labo.jp @8labo

ideot

A lifestyle store in Shibuya's Kamiya-cho offering classical yet modern and sophisticated items that are undefined by genres, eras, countries or borders and evoke a contemporary air.

URL : www.ideot.net @ideot_net

VOIRY STORE

GENERAL STORE is nestled in a quiet residential area in Meguro and stocked in an orderly fashion, like a booth in an American gas station, a school's purchasing department or a small household goods store. The store's original products and clothing such as aprons, bags and boots are available here.

URL : voiry.tokyo @voirystore

Royal Gardener's Club

Royal Gardeners Club was established by a company with a leading share of the domestic market for garden sprinkler products and water purifiers. Committed to quality manufacturing, the company deals mainly in gardening products that have a sense of the warmth that comes from handcrafting, despite being industrial products. Their shop in Jiyugaoka is run in collaboration with La terre, a women-only gardening collective. Apart from selling cut flowers, flower seedlings and gardening products, they offer advice on garden maintenance.

URL : www.rgc.tokyo @royal_gardeners_club

menui

This basket store has two branches in Kichijoji. In the Tokyu-ura store, they offer basket weaving workshops as well as stocking baskets in different materials and sizes from various countries. The Nakamichi Dori store carries miscellaneous goods and accessories along with clothing.

URL : menui.jp @menui_
　　　　　　　@menui_nakamichi

ROUSSEAU

A brand of items made of glass by Akane Nakayama. Cutting each piece of glass by hand, Nakayama draws inspiration from the orderly beauty of plants, minerals and the natural world to make vases, mirrors, glass cases and other items that allow us to enjoy the beauty of nature's forms in our daily lives.

URL : rousseau.jp   [○] @rousseau_____

Aki Hagino

Aki Hagino discovered the charm of macramé while in America and Australia. Her work centers mainly around the production of interior goods which are made by repeating simple patterns. She is based in Niigata.

URL : ronronear.theshop.jp   [○] @tami_designs

Midori no Zakka-ya

Simply adding greenery to your favorite miscellaneous items will make them even cuter! Midori no Zakka-ya stocks a huge range of natural and junk-shop style items along with the greenery that will work perfectly with them to make things cuter. Their offer is "a living space with greenery."

URL : midorinozakkaya.com   [○] @midorinozakkaya

"Books to Span the East and West"

Tuttle Publishing was founded in 1832 in the small New England town of Rutland, Vermont (USA). Our core values remain as strong today as they were then—to publish best-in-class books which bring people together one page at a time. In 1948, we established a publishing office in Japan—and Tuttle is now a leader in publishing English-language books about the arts, languages and cultures of Asia. The world has become a much smaller place today and Asia's economic and cultural influence has grown. Yet the need for meaningful dialogue and information about this diverse region has never been greater. Over the past seven decades, Tuttle has published thousands of books on subjects ranging from martial arts and paper crafts to language learning and literature—and our talented authors, illustrators, designers and photographers have won many prestigious awards. We welcome you to explore the wealth of information available on Asia at www.tuttlepublishing.com.

Published by Tuttle Publishing, an imprint of Periplus Editions (HK) Ltd.

www.tuttlepublishing.com

(Kurashi no Zukan Green : 6312-3)
©2020 Ryusuke Sakaino / Ayanas
Original Japanese edition published by SHOEISHA Co.,Ltd.
English translation rights arranged with SHOEISHA Co.,Ltd. through JAPAN UNI AGENCY, INC..
English translation copyright © 2022 by Periplus Editions (HK) Ltd.
Translated from Japanese by Leeyong Soo

ISBN 978-0-8048-5509-9

Staff (Original Japanese edition)
Design Yui Yamashiro (surmometer inc.)
DTP Yuji Kobayashi
Illustrations Ashika Zuan
Text (Part 3) Takako Ishishima
Editing Akane Koga
Author Ryusuke Sakaino/AYANAS
Publisher Mikio Sasaki

Distributed by:

North America, Latin America & Europe
Tuttle Publishing
364 Innovation Drive
North Clarendon
VT 05759-9436 U.S.A.
Tel: (802) 773-8930
Fax: (802) 773-6993
info@tuttlepublishing.com
www.tuttlepublishing.com

Asia Pacific
Berkeley Books Pte. Ltd.
3 Kallang Sector, #04-01
Singapore 349278
Tel: (65) 6741-2178
Fax: (65) 6741-2179
inquiries@periplus.com.sg
www.tuttlepublishing.com

25 24 23 22
10 9 8 7 6 5 4 3 2 1

Printed in Malaysia
2203TO